What Farmers Read and Like

WHAT FARMERS READ AND LIKE

A record of experiments with readership
on *Wallaces Farmer* and *Wisconsin Agriculturist,*
1938–1961

DONALD R. MURPHY

Iowa State University Press, *Ames,* Iowa

DONALD R. MURPHY joined the staff of *Wallaces Farmer*
(Des Moines, Iowa) in 1919. He was acting editor 1933–
46, in the period when Henry A. Wallace in Washington,
D.C. was carried on the masthead as "Editor on leave
of absence." Murphy continued to serve as editor, 1946–
1955. After retirement as editor in 1955, he became director of editorial research, 1955–60 and later contribut-
ing editor, 1961–. He was also, 1940–57, director of editorial research for *Wisconsin Agriculturist* (Racine, Wisconsin). Iowa State University gave him an award for "dis-
tinguished service to technical journalism" in 1955. In
1957, the American Association of Agricultural College
Editors gave him the Reuben Brigham Award "for meritorious service to journalism." His articles on readership
have appeared in *Journalism Quarterly, Printers' Ink* and
Advertising Age. From 1945 to 1955, he was chairman of
the agriculture committee of the National Planning Association and vice-chairman since 1955.

© 1962 by The Iowa State University Press,
Composed and printed at Ames, Iowa, U.S.A.

Library of Congress Catalog Card Number 62–9118

Introduction

THE MAGAZINE WORLD is a hazardous one. A sure path to failure is to publish the same magazine this year that pleased last year's readers. Not only do needs and interests change, the audience itself changes as old readers depart and new ones take their place.

What every magazine seeks is a path of reason — neither a strict traditionalism nor a nervous pattern of change for its own sake.

Is there a place for research in this unending quest? Can cold statistics and experimentation be used without crippling that spirit of originality that a lively, living magazine must have? Don Murphy believes they can, and he has done much to prove his point.

Murphy's consuming interest in research as an editorial tool dates back to the early 'thirties. His regular readership and opinion polls began at *Wallaces Farmer* in 1938 and at *Wisconsin Agriculturist* in 1940. They are the oldest sample surveys in the farm magazine field, and some of the oldest for any newspaper or magazine.

Critics of editorial research claim that readership

studies necessarily look to the past instead of the future. For the most part they are used to tell which of several alternatives is least desirable. They cannot by themselves create or invent new and better choices.

These are criticisms I am sure Don Murphy and his colleagues would readily accept. Surveys and experiments can give the skilled editor a particular kind of tested information to supplement his other resources. They cannot tell him how to be creative.

Yet Murphy has, in fact, been strikingly creative. The magazines under his influence have developed an extremely effective writing style — clear, simple, and direct. They use larger and more open type faces. Layouts are clearer and more straightforward. There is increased recognition of a kind of article that before did not even have a name — "dirt copy," which tackles head-on the urgent and immediate problems of farm families.

In two remarkable ways Murphy has shown his concern for the values and methods of the true scholar.

First, he has continuously developed his competence and knowledge of research techniques and has applied them ruthlessly to his own ideas and hopes. Preconceptions have not shaped his results, and he has not been afraid to say "I was wrong" or "I don't know."

Second, he has followed a policy rare in modern commercial journalism: the results of his work have been published freely and openly. Competitors are free to examine his methods, his reasoning, and his conclusions. The result has been a wholesome and continuing discussion of editorial research among his fellow farm magazine editors for nearly thirty years.

Don Murphy believes that this book highlights the important aspects of his work. In fact, the report is quite incomplete without a look at the two farm magazines with which he worked so closely. Besides the other visible marks of his presence, he has left them a valuable tradition of using research creatively and imaginatively.

Another chapter missing from this book must be read in the other American farm magazines — Murphy's competitors, if you will. His influence upon them is indisputable. His own earnest spirit of inquiry, and his willingness to share his ideas with others, have stirred up among farm magazines a refreshing spirit of self-scrutiny and a heightened concern about the reader and his needs. The credit is not Murphy's alone, but he has been an unfailing source of encouragement and support.

It is a pleasure to pay tribute to such a worthwhile service.

BRYANT E. KEARL

*Chairman, Department of
Agricultural Journalism,
College of Agriculture,
University of Wisconsin*

What This Book Is About

ON WALLACES FARMER AND WISCONSIN AGRICULTURIST, we've been testing readership for over 20 years. We started in Iowa (*Wallaces Farmer*) in 1938; in Wisconsin (*Wisconsin Agriculturist*) in 1940.

Opinion measurement on current affairs (Gallup and Roper style) started at the same time.

In over 20 years, *what have we learned about farm response to editorial and advertising copy?* This book is a summary of some of the high points of this experience.

The book was designed in the first place as a legacy from the author to his associates on *Wallaces Farmer, Wisconsin Agriculturist* and *Prairie Farmer*. The experiments may also interest editors of other publications, advertisers, advertising agencies, students of journalism and marketing and any others who deal with farm audiences in the Middle West.

I hope this publication may also stimulate others to write down and publish results of their own experiments. Much more work is being done in this field than is generally recognized, but far too little gets into a permanent record. Research men are busy; editors are loaded down with other chores and sometimes publishers feel that it is unwise to give away what they think are trade secrets.

For details on survey methods and reports, turn to Chapters 15 and 16. When sources are not given in the notes, the data reported come from the files of the Research Department, *Wallaces Farmer* and *Wisconsin Agriculturist*.

Two cautions are stressed throughout the book. They are repeated here for emphasis:

1. These experiments deal with farm audiences in Iowa and Wisconsin. We have no data of our own on other readers. However, experiments in other states indicate that most Middle Western farmers and many non-farmers respond in somewhat the same way as do Iowa and Wisconsin farm people.

2. Tastes change. What was true of copy in 1940 may not be true in 1960. Emphasis in the book is therefore given to fairly recent experiments.

In 20 years, we have reported frequently on results of editorial research. Other publications have used our results; we have borrowed from others. The art — or science — of communication has thus been advanced.

While the author has been in charge of editorial research on both *Wallaces Farmer* and *Wisconsin Agriculturist* from 1938 through 1960, the contributions of others have been great. Clifford Gregory, then associate publisher of *Wallaces Farmer*, made the policy decision in 1938 that started this work. On the *Wisconsin Agriculturist*, David Klinger, W. C. Voskuil, Ralph S. Yohe, Douglas Sorenson, and Rosemary Reid have, at different times, contributed much to these experiments. On *Wallaces Farmer*, Arthur T. Thompson, Richard Pommrehn, Richard Albrecht, Leon Thompson, and David Bryant have been active in this field. Jean Ginsberg and

Dorothy Taylor, editorial assistants at *Wallaces Farmer,* kept the records which made this report possible. Clara Bucka's work on the index was invaluable.

Looking ahead, Richard Pommrehn, director of research for the three papers, will continue this experimental work. Richard Albrecht, editor of *Wallaces Farmer,* and Ralph Yohe, editor of *Wisconsin Agriculturist,* will continue to contribute to the research program.

We owe a great deal to professional workers in the field of research. Special thanks go to Norman Strand, Arnold King and Raymond Jessen of the Statistical Laboratory, Iowa State University at Ames. We are indebted also to many workers in schools of journalism, particularly Robert Jones of the University of Minnesota, Charles Swanson, formerly of the University of Iowa, Ralph O. Nafziger and Bryant Kearl of the University of Wisconsin, Wilbur Schramm of Stanford University and Kenneth Marvin, Rodney Fox and Harry Heath of the Iowa State University at Ames. Dr. Louis Bean's advice has often stimulated our research. Our friends in the Association for Public Opinion Research and the Association for Education in Journalism have also been helpful.

This manuscript has been helped by critical reading and suggestions by several of those named above, principally Pommrehn, Albrecht, Yohe, Sorenson and Miss Reid. I have also profited by the suggestions of Dr. D. B. Murphy. The errors that remain are, of course, mine.

DONALD R. MURPHY

Table of Contents

1.

Using Research in Farm Publications

How does a farm paper happen to get started on research in the field of readership? Probably because a farm paper editor is likely to think in terms of experiments. Experiment station data on corn yields and hog feeding are the editor's daily diet. Why not apply the same methods to readers?

The only surprising thing about readership surveys in farm papers is that they came so late. It has been said, "Without readership surveys a farm paper editor is like a farmer who throws feed through a hole in the fence to hogs he never sees. He doesn't know whether they eat the feed or reject it. He doesn't know whether the hogs are gaining or losing."

Henry A. Wallace, from 1904 until he left *Wallaces Farmer* for Washington in 1933, was continually running tests on different strains of corn. Why not use similar methods on readership?

"We must get at it," said Wallace. But the actual work came after his time. What Wallace had done was to make the staff alert to the experimental approach to any problem.

"Ted" Gallup, working in Des Moines on reader-ship surveys in the 'twenties, started many people think-ing about experiments of this kind. The Gallup and Roper opinion surveys in the election of 1936 helped to emphasize these possibilities.

It was 1938 before *Wallaces Farmer* started the *Wallaces Farmer* Poll and began to report on farm at-titudes on elections and — more important to the paper — about farm reading habits.

Some editors insisted that readership surveys were not needed and that letters to the editor would give a picture of farm response to copy. We checked this sev-eral times. For instance, we asked farm people through the poll about their views on social security for farmers. A big majority approved. At the same time, we checked the letters on the subject. The letters only gave a 50-50 break to social security.

Ballots printed in the paper and sent in by readers also proved to be misleading. *Prairie Farmer* ran an ex-periment along this line and checked mailed-in-ballots against a personal interview survey. The two failed to match.

What *Wallaces Farmer* did, therefore, was to set up a polling system using a sample of around 400 inter-views (200 men and 200 women) to check readership. The sample was distributed over the state according to the economic regions as defined by the U.S. Depart-ment of Agriculture. Interviews were made by farm women trained by the *Wallaces Farmer* staff.

What do we mean by readership? If the respondent (any adult on a farm into whose mailbox the publication is delivered) said that he remembered reading the issue in question and could identify one or more items as having been read, he was classified as a reader.

After a respondent was identified as a reader, the key question by the interviewer on each page of the issue was, "Did you HAPPEN to see or read anything on this page?" The word HAPPEN is stressed to support the interviewer's opening statement that there is nothing especially virtuous about readership. We do not want the non-reader of an article to feel guilty about being a non-reader.

The respondent's answer on any page is likely to fall into one or more of the classes below. In the first place, he will have a page score. Either he read or saw nothing on the page, or he did notice something. If he did notice something, he is given a score for "Any This Page."

Some possible reports on advertisements and articles are listed below:

Advertisement	Article
1. **Nothing**	1. **Nothing**
2. **"Any This Ad"** — Respondent has seen or read one or more features of this particular advertisement	2. **"Any This Article"** — Respondent has looked at head, picture, or read something in the article
3. **"Seen"** — Respondent has looked at a picture or a head	3. **"Seen"** — Respondent has looked at picture or head
4. **"Read Some"** — Respondent has read less than half of a particular piece of copy	4. **"Read Some"** — Respondent has read less than half of article
5. **"Read Most"** — Respondent has read half or more of a particular piece of copy	5. **"Read Most"** — Respondent has read half or more of article

An advertisement, therefore, might have one score for "Any This Ad;" another for "Seen" on the head; another "Seen" on the illustration; another score for

"Read Some" on a block of sales copy; another for "Read Most" on the same block of sales copy. Scores for men and women are always reported separately.

In the tables that follow, the figures given are always percentages of the sample used. When the men's sample is 200 cases, a score of 50 per cent, of course, means that 100 men responded in the way indicated. In split runs the A sample and the B sample each includes 100 men and 100 women. A score of 50 per cent means that 50 cases responded in the way indicated.

On opinion polls, the sample is larger and not so constant. On breakdowns of readership surveys, the sub-samples are smaller; and they vary. In each case, however, when there are exceptions to the rule noted in the paragraph above, the sample size is given.

While readership surveys (except in a few early surveys) always use a constant sample of 200 men and 200 women, opinion polls vary in size. The opinion sample ranges from 400 to 700 interviews in each state.

Opinion polls, of course, deal with a sample of all the farm men and women in each state. Readership surveys deal with a sample of the subscribers in each state.

One of the hazards of setting up your own survey machinery is that your interviewers may show a bias in favor of the paper that hires them. We tried to offset this in training sessions to point out necessity for keeping absolutely impartial approaches and comments.

We also checked our survey results against surveys made by independent operators. The Continuing Study of Farm Papers, conducted by the Advertising Research Foundation, ran a survey in the September 20, 1947 issue of *Wallaces Farmer.* (1)

Our survey crews checked the same issue independently. Was the *Wallaces Farmer* Poll getting higher readership scores than the Continuing Study? At our request, Professor Roscoe Giffin of Iowa State University went over the results and found that with men, in six cases our scores were higher than the Continuing Study. In 49 cases our scores were lower. In one case, they were exactly the same. With women, in eight cases our scores were higher than the Continuing Study and in 54 cases, lower. In one case, the score was the same.

Starch makes regular checks on readership of *Wallaces Farmer* and *Wisconsin Agriculturist*. Starch scores, as a rule, tend to run a little higher than ours, especially on ads. There is some difficulty in comparison because surveys are made in different months. In 1959, however, we had a readership survey of *Wisconsin Agriculturist* in October, and Starch had one of the same magazine in November.

Of 11 editorial departments, the Read Most scores compared as follows:

	OUR SURVEY		STARCH	
Read Most	Men	Women	Men	Women
Average of 11 departments . .	34%	36%	38.3%	34.0%

This seems a reasonably close fit. On the whole, it does not seem that the readership scores in our surveys are biased because our interviewers do the work. It may help impartiality that our interviewers are trained in pre-election polls and know that errors from bias will show up.

A series of surveys by the Statistical Laboratory of Iowa State University at Ames gave us further information. These surveys, in 1947, 1951 and 1955, told where farmers go to get information on different subjects. (2) They gave us a better picture of our subscribers, what they were like, and what kind of subjects interested them.

* * *

It should be kept in mind that throughout this book, the readership scores are given with readers of the issue as a base. Non-readers are also measured but, of course, in a different way.

A reader, as noted above, is any adult in the subscriber sample, who recalls one or more items in the issue. A non-reader is any adult in the sample of subscriber homes who reported that he or she had read nothing in the current issue.

While readership studies are built around readers of the current issue, the non-reader is also important. Professor Bryant Kearl, head of the Department of Agricultural Journalism at the University of Wisconsin, said, "A description of non-readers could be one of the most useful parts of a readership survey." (3) Chapter 9 goes into this.

* * *

What did we learn from the early readership surveys? Perhaps the first thing was to avoid jumps. We found that when an article started on page 10 and jumped to page 50, many readers were lost.

This seems obvious enough now. Since 1938, most publications in our field have abolished the jump. It is still used in magazines which use extra-long articles or stories. In these cases, however, the opening page or spread, featuring a big illustration and not much type, is really only an expanded plug.

In our early experiments, we found that we lost about 30 per cent of our readers when we had a sizable jump. If the jump were dressed up with a cut and a strong head, the loss was cut down.

In March, 1944, we ran another test. An article starting on page one scored 61.1 for men there; the runover on page 21 scored 49.7. Somewhat later, we tried starting an article on the right-hand page and continuing it on the following left-hand page. This lost readers, too.

A detailed report on this point came from the University of Iowa in 1958. Six articles in one publication started on the right-hand page and were continued on the following left-hand page. These runovers lost, on the average, 49 per cent with men and 25 per cent with women.

The answer, so far as we were concerned, seemed plain enough back in 1940. Complete every article on the page on which it starts. If the article is longer, let it run from a left-hand page to a right-hand one — but no farther. This policy, of course, meant more editing and more rewriting. But most farm publications, including ours, don't do as much desk work on copy as they should anyway.

* * *

Readership scores were helpful in showing us which kind of copy was likely to be read and whether an article appealed to young readers, to old readers, to men, to women, to big farmers, to small farmers, to owners, to tenants, and so on.

What these surveys lacked was a definite comparison between different layouts, uses of color, styles of cuts, placements of copy and other points. We could say that Ad A, in January, scored 40 per cent Noted with men, and that Ad B, in March, on the same kind of product, scored 30 per cent Noted with men. But did that mean Ad A was any better? A snow storm in March, a thaw in January, might have changed reader response to the two issues.

To give a fair test to editorial copy or to ads, it seemed necessary to expose this copy to readers at exactly the same time. This meant using what we called a "split run."

The term "split run" has since changed its meaning for many. Now it often indicates that Magazine A will run special copy in, for example, Illinois and Indiana. The same pages will carry special and different copy for Ohio and Pennsylvania.

Our "split run" goes back instead to the practice of newspapers with mail-order ads. With newspapers, every other one that came off the press would have different copy. Ad A would go to half the readers; Ad B to the other half. The results were measured by coupon return.

This worked well for mail-order ads. It was no help to other kinds of advertisers, to whom coupon returns were not important.

What we did was to set up two samples in each state. Think of Iowa, with its 99 counties, as a checkerboard. We sent A copies to the red counties, and B copies to the black counties.

Actually, we never used this big a sample. Ordinarily, we interviewed in about 20 A counties and 20 B counties. The interviews in the A counties were distributed proportionately among the five economic regions of the state. The same was done in the B counties. We ended up with two samples, closely matched — 100 interviews with men and 100 interviews with women in the A counties and the same number in the B counties.

* * *

We tried our first split in 1946 to test readability levels. When Rudolph Flesch published his doctoral dissertation at Columbia on the subject back in 1944, we got one of the copies and began to wonder about its applicability to our problems. With his *Art of Plain Talk* (Harpers, 1946) we settled down to test his theories.

The Flesch hypothesis was that copy with short sentences, short words (few affixes) and "personal" words would attract and hold more readers than copy with longer sentences, longer words and fewer "personal" words.

In the March 1, 1946 issue of *Wallaces Farmer*, we ran three splits based on the Flesch formula. The main thing we learned from this was that we were shooting too high. We moved — in Flesch's words — from a seventh grade level to a sixth grade level. Our readers didn't notice the difference.

Only when we moved to a much simpler level did the new copy take hold. The Flesch index of 1.5 seemed to increase readership. What did this mean? The copy would average around 12 words per sentence, 20 affixes for 100 words and 10 personal references per 100 words.

In November, 1946, we tried again. This time we split three men's articles and one woman's article.

Remember that nothing was changed except the

style. The head, the illustration and the theme had not been altered. The copy was edited only to get different levels of readability in terms of the Flesch index.

In the four splits, the low Flesch copy ranged from 1.11 to 1.76. The high Flesch counts ranged from 2.48 to 4.27.

Of the eight comparisons (using men and women for each split), we couldn't use three. On two pieces of copy designed for men, the women's score was too low to provide any answers. On one piece of copy the men's scores were too low for us to use.

Of the five split comparisons, where the number of readers was fairly high, one piece of men's copy showed a loss of 9.4 per cent for the low Flesch score. With the other four, increases ranged from 7.3 to 66 per cent for the low Flesch score over the high score. (4)

We have since tried similar splits in *Wisconsin Agriculturist* and in later issues of *Wallaces Farmer*. Experiments at the University of Iowa made another check. (5) The results seemed clear enough. Other things being equal, simple language scored high.

Does this mean we try to write for morons? Not at all. An experiment at Iowa State University at Ames threw some light on this delusion. A split, using Flesch scores, was tried out on faculty members and students. Presumably the faculty members were the intellectuals. Yet the simpler Flesch copy did better with the faculty than with the students.

Why? The copy was in a field of more interest to the students than to the faculty. When readers are excited about a subject, they'll read difficult copy, printed in small type. When their feelings are neutral, they'll respond better to readable copy. If you can pick sub-jects of overwhelming interest, you can write badly and get away with it. Nobody is that good a picker. It is better to assume that some of your readers may be indifferent.

As members of our staff promptly pointed out, you can write very bad copy that has a good Flesch score. "I see a cat. Do you see a cat?" scores well on the Flesch index.

To avoid disasters like this, our rule was to write the copy as well as we could. Remember what the teacher said in English 1 — short, easily understood words, action verbs and not too many adjectives, speci-fic and colorful descriptions, questions and names.

After writing — and often after publishing — we went over the copy with the Flesch index. The staff noted the scores and sometimes remembered them next time.

The extent of improvement in style may be meas-ured in this way. Before we started testing, we took our usual copy (around 3.5 Flesch) and edited to bring it down to 1.5. After some months of education, we found that our usual copy was around 1.5 Flesch. To get a split, we had to edit to bring one version up to 3.5.

One source of confusion in using the Flesch index is the fact that the author changed his measuring de-vice. In the earlier Flesch scoring system the low score (note 1.5 above) was the best. In *The Art of Readable Writing* Flesch uses a measuring stick called "Reading Ease." (6) Here the high score is the best. The Reading Ease score is based on syllables per 100 and on words per sentence.

A meritorious Reading Ease score would be 80 (much like the old Flesch index of 1.5). This would mean 12 words per sentence and 134 syllables per 100 words. A "difficult" Reading Ease score might be around 40 with 20 words per sentence and 173 syllables per 100 words.

Just to see if readability (in Flesch terms) was still important, we ran a split in *Wallaces Farmer* for January 16, 1960 on the article entitled "USDA Studies Soil Acidity" (Figures 1.2 and 1.3). Following is the Reading Ease Index and the resulting scores for men:

	A (Difficult)	B (Easy)
Words per sentence . . .	16	13
Syllables per 100 words .	170	141
Reading Ease Index . .	56.0	74.6
Read Some on copy . . .	32.0%	47.0%
Read Most	30.0%	43.0%

It may help to show what happened here if we quote the lead from each version of the copy: (A was a USDA release)

Version A — 56 Reading Ease

The strong trend to heavier nitrogen fertilization, coupled with reduced use of lime over the past decade, is making our nation's soil more acid. That's why USDA has expanded its research into the problem of acidity.

Version B — 74 Reading Ease

Are you planning to put a lot of nitrogen fertilizer on your fields this spring? If you are, make sure also that you've spread enough lime on these same fields.

How do you determine "Reading Ease," according to Flesch? His *Art of Readable Writing* has a time-saving chart. The Flesch formula — if you don't use the chart — goes like this:

Multiply the average sentence length by 1.015;

Multiply the number of syllables per 100 words by 0.846;

Subtract the sum of the two items above from 206.835.

What is left is Reading Ease.

It is a good deal easier to remember that you can get a Reading Ease score of 75 — which is pretty good — in the following ways:

15 words per sentence and 138 syllables per 100 words

or

12 words per sentence and 142 syllables per 100 words

or

18 words per sentence and 134 syllables per 100 words.

On the other hand, if your Reading Ease score falls below 50, you are probably losing readers. A score of 50 can be obtained in the following ways:

18 words per sentence and 164 syllables per 100 words

or

20 words per sentence and 162 syllables per 100 words

or

25 words per sentence and 156 syllables per 100 words.

It is still a good idea to get a copy of the book and use the Flesch chart.

If you are hitting somewhere between 60 and 80 on the Reading Ease Index, you are doing fairly well. But, note that we have had very high scoring copy — Read Most scores of 60 per cent or better — that had a Flesch rating of 65. And we have had low scoring copy — Read Most of 30 per cent or less — that had a Flesch rating of 80.

All this means is that subject matter is always more important than style. A hog article, in Iowa, will always outscore a sheep article. But a sheep article with a Flesch index of 80 will usually outscore another sheep article with a Flesch index of 55 or less.

There are, of course, other methods, and excellent ones, of scoring readability. We have stuck to Flesch because we happened to start with it and because it has stood up under split-run testing.

This was our start in split-run testing. I have reported it in some detail because it illustrates the methods used in many later experiments. The split-run device has thrown light on many problems in advertising and editorial customs.

Each split-run reader-interest survey for some years has had five to seven splits with ads and the same number or more with editorial matter. Some of these proved that the differences we expected did not exist. Some showed a sharp reader response to a change of layout or copy.

Succeeding chapters go into detail on some of the things that advertisers and editors learned.

Figure 1.1

Editorial Page

Page Score

80.5% Men

55.0% Women

Who Reads Editorials?

Do subscribers read the editorial page? What kind of subscribers?

Above is the first editorial page (*Wallaces* runs a spread of two) in a fall issue of *Wallaces Farmer*. Men read more editorials than women. As you might expect, the men's first choice was the editorial on hog prices, with a Read Most of 54.5 per cent.

Young men (21–34 years) read about as much as older men (50 and up). Farm men with gross incomes of $10,000 a year read more than men with smaller incomes.

Wallaces Farmer, November 19, 1960

[25]

USDA studies soil acidity

Research is intended to show how acidity can cut yields

THE STRONG trend to heavier nitrogen fertilization, coupled with reduced use of lime over the past decade, is making our nation's soils more acid. That's why USDA has expanded its research into the problem of acidity.

While these experiments are not being conducted on Iowa soils, the results may prove helpful to Iowa agronomists. Scientists have taken only the first few steps in fully understanding soil-plant interactions. When they unlock enough of this information, fertilizers and fertilizer use can be adapted more closely to plant needs. And plants can be bred to make better use of their environment.

More than 50 field experiments on 23 agriculturally important soil types are now being conducted in cooperation with state experiment stations to fill in the gaps of our understanding of how acidity decreases yield. These same soils are also studied under uniform environmental conditions in greenhouse and laboratory to learn why they behave as they do.

Altho this research is only in its second year, it has already given some interesting leads. For example, alfalfa was grown in the greenhouse on two silt loams that showed the same lime requirement when tested by accepted soil tests.

When limed, one soil gave a 400-percent increase in yield but the other gave only a 25-percent increase. Understanding the reason for such differences in behavior among soils would be one of the keys to accurate prediction of lime requirements.

Toxic concentrations of manganese and aluminum are probably the most common cause of poor plant growth in acid soils. There is no doubt in the scientists' minds that acidity is serious, but there are still questions as to how it causes known reactions:

Is aluminum or manganese toxicity the more important problems?

Under what conditions and for which crops and soils are these toxicities of particular significance?

What are the interactions of nutrients such as phosphorus with toxic levels of aluminum and manganese?

How and to what extent does organic matter alleviate the toxicity of these elements? What are the critical levels of these elements in important crops?

Soil acidity is a serious soil management problem in the cornbelt, says ARS soil scientist R. W. Pearson.

From 1947 to 1957, the use of nitrogen fertilizer over the nation jumped from less than a million tons to 2.3 million tons a year. But the use of limestone dropped over a third, from 28 million to 18 million tons in 1954, and had only increased back to 22 million by 1958. Some 80 million tons are estimated to be needed annually to maintain optimum soil reaction.

Figure 1.2

A

Read Most

Men 30%

No, They Aren't the Same!

The two articles here look alike, but they score differently. They have the same head, the same theme and the same structure. But they differ in the number of long words and long sentences.

In a series of splits, of which this is the most recent, copy with short sentences and short words has been shown to help readership.

Figure 1.3

B

Read Most

Men 43%

USDA studies
soil acidity

Research is intended to show how acidity can cut yields

ARE YOU planning to put a lot of nitrogen fertilizer on your fields this spring? If you are, make sure also that you've spread enough lime on these same fields.

Sour soils take a lot of the vigor out of fertilizers—especially nitrogen. Unless a field is limed, you won't get anywhere near full value out of your fertilizer.

Cornbelt soils are getting more sour. At the same time that fertilizer use has gone up, use of lime has gone down. In Iowa, for instance, there was a 54 percent drop in the use of limestone from 1957 to 1958.

Nationally, the same thing is happening. From 1947 to 1957, the use of limestone dropped over a third. At the same time, the use of nitrogen fertilizer more than doubled.

To keep the nation's soil sweet, farmers need to spread around 80 million tons of limestone a year. In 1958, only 22 million tons were spread.

Most farmers know that sour soils make it harder to get a stand of legumes. Not all realize that the value of their fertilizer may be cut heavily when applied to sour soils.

To find out just what happens to crops in sour soils, a number of experiments are being carried on. Over the nation, 50 different field experiments are being carried on with 23 soil types.

Some of the answers so far just raise additional questions. In one greenhouse experiment, two silt loams were tested. Apparently the two had the same lime requirements. But see what happened:

When limed, one soil gave a 400 percent increase in yield. The other gave only a 25 percent. Nobody yet is sure why.

Two of the villains in sour soils are probably manganese and aluminum. Sour soils usually have too much of these minerals. Crop growth slows down.

But does manganese do most of the damage? Or is aluminum a major culprit?

What happens when you add phosphorus to a sour soil overloaded with manganese and aluminum?

Does it help sour soil of this kind to plow under green manure or to add a lot of barnyard manure? Or does such action make things worse?

These are some of the questions scientists are asking themselves. No final answers have been determined yet.

In the meantime, it does seem certain that sour soils don't get the big benefits out of nitrogen fertilizer. When you plan your program for 1960 crops, you may want to use lime as well as nitrogen.

Tho the research is only in its second year, many interesting leads have already been produced. In the future, this research should answer lots of questions on soil acidity.

Here is the difference in the two pieces of copy:

	A	B
Words per sentence	16	13
Syllables per 100 words . . .	170	141

Editing A copy to the B standard raised the Read Most score for men fom 30 in A to 43 in B. Read Some scores showed a similar gain.

Wallaces Farmer, January 16, 1960

Figure 1.4

Food Page

Page Score

Women 90.5%

Recipes Pull Women In

Farm women continue to read food copy, especially if there is a local angle. This Home Department lead page addressed to "Young Cooks" actually scored almost as well with older women as it did with younger ones.

	21–34 years	50 and up
Read Most	84.8%	76.3%

The photo (upper right) of the Wisconsin farm girl, Karen Ulness of Manitowoc County, drew the attention of 90 per cent of the women readers of the issue.

Wisconsin Agriculturist, April 15, 1961

2.

Front Covers That Attract Readers

A FARM PAPER EDITOR is in some ways like the publisher of a picture magazine who tries to build up his newsstand sales. But the farm paper's newsstand is the table in the front room where the mail is dumped. Which paper or which magazine in that collection will catch the eye of the possible reader?

We have to keep in mind that in Iowa half of the farm homes take four or more farm publications and three or more general non-farm magazines. Wisconsin farmers read a little less avidly, but the competition is still severe. And in both states, almost everybody takes a newspaper and has a radio and a television set.

The non-reader problem is a major one for an editor. And it ties directly into the use of the front cover.

How do we define a non-reader? He is any adult who lives in a family where the paper is received and who doesn't read the issue being surveyed.

Farm papers are not the only ones that have trouble.

A good co-op newspaper, the *Midland Cooperator,* surveyed by the U. S. Department of Agriculture, had 44 per cent of its possible men readers in the non-reader class, and 33 per cent of the women. (1) A well-edited house organ of a feed company reported one internal survey which showed a non-reader problem of somewhat the same nature.

If page one demands attention, the potential non-reader may pick up the copy. If the bait is good enough, he may open up the paper and read something inside.

When you look over the score for non-readers, you realize how important page one is. *Wallaces Farmer,* for instance, has a 20 issue mean of 14.5 per cent men non-readers and 17.9 per cent women non-readers. The *Wisconsin Agriculturist* has a mean over 19 issues of 16.8 per cent men non-readers and 16.1 per cent women non-readers.

Remember that a 20 per cent non-reader figure does not mean that 20 per cent of the households on the subscription list sample had no readers of the issue surveyed. The non-reader figure deals with individuals, not with households. In visiting 10 households, one of our interviewers may find 16 readers and four non-readers (20 per cent non-readers), but he may also find that the 16 readers are so distributed that there is, at least, one reader in every household.

The Advertising Research Foundation in its "Continuing Study of Farm Publications" found that *Wallaces Farmer* had 1.76 readers per copy in spite of the fact that the non-reader percentage for that issue was fairly high. (2)

One way to try to find out which cover is doing

the job is to check non-readers. *Wallaces Farmer* did best with men in March 1954 and March 1952. In the 1954 issue, the non-reader score was 6.8 per cent. In the 1952 issue, the non-reader score was 9.2. What kind of cover was used in each case?

Each had a timely theme appropriate to the month and the season, a big head playing up this theme, a picture to illustrate it and a caption written in article style. In each case, plugs were added.

In March 1954, the page scored 94 with men; the copy scored 75 per cent Read Most for men; the head, not scored, was "Got Manure Hauled?" Four plugs, all aimed at men, scored Read Some 63 for men and 32 for women.

Did these two covers score high because they were effective or because farmers do more reading in March? There is some evidence that these March covers did not score high simply because they were in March. We have had some low March scores. As reported later, we have had high scores in September, April and November.

Yet this does illustrate the value of the split run. Any effect of the season on the score is wiped out when we have a cover split. On the November 6, 1954 issue of *Wisconsin Agriculturist* the shift from a dairy cover (A) to a farm family cover (B) showed a marked difference among women in favor of B. November weather made no difference. A and B were affected the same.

In Wisconsin, we find that the lowest (therefore best) three non-reader scores for men appeared in the following issues:

March 3, 1951 (non-reader score 9.7 per cent)
November 2, 1957 (non-reader score 12 per cent)
April 2, 1960 (non-reader score 10.7 per cent on A copy).

Of these, the 1957 issue used the standard head above the cut and a somewhat weaker caption than some of our other good-scoring pages. The page score was 93 for men. The caption scored 70 for men.

The 1951 issue used a strong head also, but mortised it in the lower part of the cut. The caption was written in article style. Men scored 91 on the page and 79 on the copy.

Of these issues with a low non-reader score, only the April 2, 1960, A version broke the pattern. It had no head, a short caption, and fairly strong plugs. Score for the page was 90 for men, for the plugs 52 and for the caption 51.

This question always comes up, "Why don't we get a 100 per cent score on a cover among readers of the issue? Doesn't a farmer notice the cover when he picks it up?"

Sometimes he doesn't. A farmer may turn directly to a special department like "What's Ahead." A woman may turn to the homemaking section. Each recognizes, by the different cover, that it is a new issue, but that is as much as some respondents will report.

In the listing above, women's scores on the cover have not been given. Mostly they were poor and for a good reason. The cover often did not have anything of interest for women.

There are some exceptions. In *Wallaces Farmer* (January 7, 1959), the theme was planning gardens.

In the B version, the women's score was 89 per cent for the cover.

Another issue (January 18, 1958) had farm records as the theme with a man and woman in the picture. Scores for the picture were 85 per cent for men and also for women.

Shifting to *Wisconsin Agriculturist*, we find the April 5, 1958 issue had one of the high scoring covers. Here color was used on a dairy picture, and plugs played up with plenty of white space were put in the upper right hand corner of the picture. (It might be noted that a *Wallaces Farmer* cover using plugs in about the same position also got good plug results on this placing.)

The *Wisconsin Agriculturist* cover scored for the picture, 85 for men and 84 for women; for the plugs, 69 for men and 51 for women.

Two more *Wallaces Farmer* covers also might be noted. In March 16, 1957, there was a big head overprinted "When Neighbors Stop To Chat." The picture score was 91 and 86; the caption 74 and 59. Here the caption was mortised in the lower part of the cut.

In the September 20, 1958 issue, the head was overprinted "You Helped Buy Them," a reference to a campaign to buy gilts for flood-hit farmers. The picture scored 90.5 for men and 74.5 for women. A split on this issue showed that an expanded plug set like a caption and crowded with too little white space produced a low score.

What good are plugs? We are fairly sure that they do not help the score of the article plugged. Splits have seemed to prove this. That is why we now leave off the page number on the plug. What the plug does — if we are smart enough — is to pull readers into the issue.

An example is *Wisconsin Agriculturist,* October 3, 1959. On the cover split, we used "Harvest Time Comes to Wisconsin" as the A plug and "What Farmers Think of Khrushchev's Visit . . . Page 20" as the B plug.

The article on page 20 scored 58 per cent Read Most for men in A and 59 in B. For women, 45 in A and 45 in B.

*   *   *

What kind of material goes best on page one? After going over reader-interest surveys for a number of years in both states, there seems a fairly strong case for the following ingredients:

1. Use a timely theme for picture, head and copy. If the theme deals with a subject likely to be on the farmer's mind at the time he gets the paper, he will probably look at the issue. This is standard editorial policy for planning timely articles.

   EXAMPLE: On the October 5, 1957 *Wallaces Farmer* is a picture of a man greasing a combine. The head (below picture) is "Keep It Greased." The copy — handled like a short article — talks about soybean combining. Plugs also play up soybeans. The score for the page was 92 for men; 77 for women (Figure 2.6).

It might be noted also that the non-reader score for men in the October 5, 1957 *Wallaces Farmer* was 14.4, and for women 20.5. Yet, there was nothing on the cover for women readers. Another good cover was the September 15, 1956, *Wallaces Farmer* with the head "Feeders Moving Fast" below the cut. Copy, handled like a short article, dealt with late news on feeder shipments. Plugs hit other subjects.

2. A strong head, 42-point or bigger, seems desirable to emphasize the cover theme. This head can either be overprinted on part of the cut (provided it's that kind of a picture) or better — played up heavily under the cut.
3. The caption should be handled like a short article — large type and enough detail to stress the theme.
4. Plugs should include some references to women's copy, and should be lively enough to qualify as good bait.
5. Change the cover style from issue to issue in order to make sure that the reader knows he is getting a fresh copy. A big head can help on this — so can changes in layout.

NOTES ON COVER PAGES

Pick out the major theme for the issue, the most timely, the most important. Use a photograph that illustrates this theme and put it on page one. An example is the November 5, 1949 issue of *Wallaces Farmer*. Corn had blown down early in the fall and there was the big job of picking up fallen ears. The cover played this up and got a page score of 96.4 per cent for men and 86.7 per cent for women. The same theme was used on page five, where men had a Read Most score of 65.1 and a page score of 89.2.

* * *

A caption under the cover picture should not be too long or too tight. In the A version of the January 17, 1959 *Wallaces Farmer,* a four-line caption (Vogue 12-point) was stretched out to 47 picas. It scored badly, especially with women, against a caption set in 12-point Corona, with short lines (14 picas). The score with women in A was 49; B, 70. This was women's gardening copy.

* * *

Women and children, in a good picture, will draw men as well as women. The November 5, 1955, *Wisconsin Agriculturist* cover had a school scene in a close-up of children and teacher with a reverse head across top "How Well Can Johnny Read." There was no caption (probably a mistake) and plugs. Men scored 85.2 per cent and women 81.5 per cent for the page (Figure 2.1).

* * *

Another problem is the dirt picture vs. human interest picture. The November 6, 1954 *Wisconsin Agriculturist* ran a split of different covers. In A was a dairy picture (Bang's test) with a head "Blood Will Tell" and expanded caption. In B, was a farm family at the store buying clothes with a head "Sure Sign of Winter" and expanded caption. Both pictures did well; women gave B a little preference. Each had a big head, expanded caption and plugs. Each was timely.

	Men		Women	
	A	B	A	B
Any This Page	93.4%	95.3%	81.8%	93.5%
Picture . . .	92.0	92.9	80.9	90.7
Plugs	50.0	54.1	38.2	56.5
Caption . . .	79.2	65.9	55.4	69.4

* * *

If you want women to read the issue, play to them on the cover. In October 5, 1955 *Wallaces Farmer,* the A issue of the split had a picture of a Master Farm Homemaker. B did not have a picture of a woman. The score for the page was 96 per cent for A with women, 62 per cent for B.

Figure 2.1

Cover Page

Page Score

Men 85.2%

Women 81.5%

WISCONSIN Agriculturist AND FARMER

SERVING WISCONSIN FARM FAMILIES THROUGH 106 YEARS

Racine, Wisconsin   November 5, 1955

How Well CAN Johnny Read ?

Read what farmers say in WAAF Poll—page 18

- Stick with Stanchions? 6   • Hay from New Seeding 28
- Draftees Have a Choice   . . . 24

Covers That Pull Readers

Not every reader of an issue really looks at the cover. Some turn directly to the department they usually read. But an attractive cover can draw the attention of men and women who might otherwise be non-readers.

This *Wisconsin Agriculturist* cover did well with both men and women. It also built up an audience for the article on page 18 that was plugged by the cover and the caption. That article on Johnny and his reading habits scored 59.5 Read Most with women.

Wisconsin Agriculturist, November 5, 1955

[37]

Figure 2.2

Cover Split A

Page Score

Men 97%

Women 91%

Close-up Does Better

In this cover split on *Wallaces Farmer,* both the close-up A version and the long shot B version did well with both men and women. However, the close-up A picture not only scored higher with readers, but also had fewer non-readers among those exposed to the issue.

This cover did an unusually good job in pulling women into the issue without scaring off men. Farm children in Adair (or Pocahontas) County, Iowa, appeal to farm men and women in Iowa.

Figure 2.3

Cover Split B

Page Score

Men 86%

Women 81%

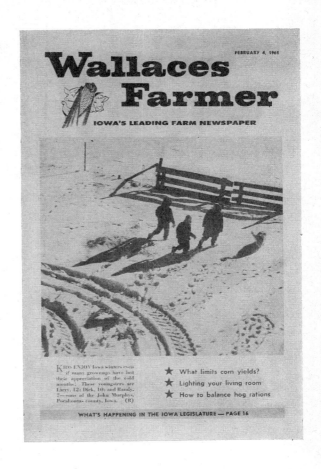

Scores for A and B follow. Note that readership held up fairly well down through the plugs at the bottom of the page.

	Men A	B	Women A	B
Any Page 1	97%	86%	91%	81%
Picture	95	85	89	90
Caption	64	61	65	51
Plugs	68	68	59	41

Wallaces Farmer, February 4, 1961

It's tough getting started in farming these
days, but youth and determination are a big
help. That's what Justine and Paul Fowler,
Winnebago county, have — along with a
belief in the value of good farm accounting.
For the full story turn to page 10.

NEW FEED GRAIN BILL
GET CORN PLANTER READY
HE FARMS ON 60 ACRES

Figure 2.4

Cover Split A

Page Score

Men 86%

Women 85%

The Headline Helped

Does it pay to use a strong head on the cover? In this
Wisconsin split, the A version uses no head; the B version
uses a head. This is the only difference.

In cutting down the number of non-readers, the B cover
(head) did much better than A with women and a little
better with men. The readership scores also give an edge to
B with men.

Figure 2.5

Cover Split B

Page Score

Men 94%

Women 83%

Young couple gets started in dairying

It's tough getting started in farming these days, but youth and determination are a big help. That's what Justine and Paul Fowler, Winnebago county, have — along with a belief in the value of good farm accounting. For the full story turn to page 10.

NEW FEED GRAIN BILL
GET CORN PLANTER READY
HE FARMS ON 60 ACRES

The head in B also pulled up the score for the caption in B. Men's scores were 52 for the caption in A and 70 in B.

The combination of picture, head and caption directed interest toward the article plugged. On page 10, this article showed a higher score in B for both men and women.

Read Some	A	B
Men	52%	64%
Women	24	33

Wisconsin Agriculturist, April 15, 1961

Figure 2.6

Cover Page

Page Score

Men 92%

Women 77%

Timely Theme Pays Off

Soybean harvesting reaches a peak in Iowa in early October. So a cover aimed at this timely theme scored well. A picture of a farmer greasing a combine (in Davis County, Iowa) scored 89 per cent for men and 77 for women.

In general, this is the pattern that has paid off in cover scores. Pick a timely theme, illustrate it with an Iowa (or Wisconsin) farmer doing something appropriate and use headline and caption to emphasize the topic.

Wallaces Farmer, October 5, 1957

3.

Does a Second Color Help?

DOES IT PAY to use a second color (yellow, red, green, orange) on a layout for editorial matter or for advertising? This question has been the subject of over 30 splits.

The answers tend to run in one direction. Most of the time, a second color — in *Wallaces Farmer* and *Wisconsin Agriculturist* — doesn't do much to help readership.

This conclusion has exasperated all of us in the office. We like the looks of a second color. We think readers should like it. Unfortunately, it appears as if they don't. We keep thinking we'll yet find a color combination that will do something substantial for readership. Perhaps we will eventually, but we haven't yet.

It should be pointed out that this conclusion should be accepted only for farm audiences in Iowa and Wisconsin and for our kind of publication. The fact is that a second color is no treat to our readers. Our papers are full of second colors — especially red. If fewer ads used a second color, the ones that do use it might show up better.

To detail all the color splits would take too much space. Following are some high points:

White letters on red. This was used by Quaker Oats in *Wisconsin Agriculturist* (November 7, 1953, page 41) in the A version. B had the same head, but black letters on white, with a red line around the head (Figures 3.7, 3.8).

Women	A (Reverse)	B (Black)
Head	23.3%	52.0%
Sales Copy (Read Most) . .	12.9	31.0

The reverse head (as in A above) has been tested by many researchers. Their conclusions, in general, agree with ours.

Head in color. This split, probably because it is easy to handle, has been tried by us more than any other.

Typical is the Nutrena ad in the *Wisconsin Agriculturist* (November 7, 1953, page 21). A put the head in red; B in black.

Men	A (Color)	B (Black)
Any This Ad	30.0%	34.5%
Head	24.3	23.8

This has been the usual experience. There is no measurable gain through using a head in color. On some splits, it seemed that the black head scored a little better.

Overprint. We have used black letters on a red screen; black on a yellow screen or a yellow solid, etc.

We did not have much luck with this, but a few splits seemed to hold some hope. Here is one:

Overprint (black on yellow) was tried in *Wallaces Farmer* (March 1, 1947). The head, "Why Work Hard at Chores" was black on yellow for A and black on white for B.

	A (Color)	B (Black)
Any This Page	**86.0%**	**80.0%**
Women	**33.7**	**19.7**

There is no difference for men, but with women, the difference is significant. Men, more interested in the article, were not impressed by the color. Women, not so much interested in the article, apparently responded to color.

This same tendency has showed up in other splits. The readers who were less interested in the copy might be lured by color or some other layout gadget. Those more interested in the copy paid no attention.

If we are trying for a dual purpose score (good with both men and women) and the article is aimed at men, color may help the women's score. If the article is aimed at women, color may help the men's score.

Does this tentative rule work with ads? Once in a while. But the evidence is stronger for editorial copy.

It makes a difference, of course, whether the overprint is imposed on a solid color or a screen. We haven't had much luck with solids; there is a tendency to smear. With red or green, the screen range has been from 40 to 60. On the whole, 50 has been the best. With yellow, a heavy screen (70) has looked the best, though we have gone as low as 50. A 50 screen with yellow, however, tends to fade out. There have been no readership splits on the different screens.

What about an overprint of black on red? In the *Wisconsin Agriculturist* (November 3, 1951, page 9), a one-column, two-line head was overprinted in black on red in B; black on white in A.

Men	A	B (Color)
Read Some	**41.1%**	**36.1%**

Unchanged copy on the same page gave the edge to B.

A heavy red border around the head was used in *Wisconsin Agriculturist* (February 20, 1954, page 6) for A. The color was taken off for B.

Men	A (Color)	B
Any This Page	**93.3%**	**93.2%**

For a test split, this copy was too attractive. It was a dairy story and pulled almost all the readers. Color made no difference here. It might have made some difference if the article had dealt with sheep or hogs, less popular than cows in Wisconsin.

Studies of 11 splits in *Wallaces Farmer* where color was used with ads were made by R. J. Pommrehn. This report deals with a variety of uses of color. None made any significant difference in the scores, except that in a few cases low scores for women on ads addressed to men were pulled up a little by color. (1)

Cornell University reports an experiment in a somewhat different field. A sample of New York dairymen were sent a leaflet on early and late cut hay and silage.

Half of the sample got this leaflet (an advance print from *Successful Farming*) in black and white; half, in four color. (2)

Apparently the black and white had as much effect as the four color. The bulletin adds this caution:

> It must be recognized that the test article used in this study had a high degree of attraction for the dairyman, since it directly affected profit. Consequently it might be expected that it would be read regardless of whether it was presented in color or in black and white. Possibly color is more important for attracting and holding attention among those for whom the item has less possibility of affecting profit.

This matches the experience of *Wallaces Farmer* and *Wisconsin Agriculturist*.

A yellow screen was tried out behind black type of "What's Ahead" in *Wallaces Farmer* (September 20, 1958).

Men	A (Color)	B
Read Some	63%	51%
Read Most	57	41

This made black on yellow look hopeful. But two later splits with black charts on yellow showed no advantage. We are inclined to say that black type on a yellow screen probably has some advantages but that the point needs further testing.

Red screen as background for department heads was tried out several times. The best showing was with "Country Air" *Wallaces Farmer* (September 20, 1958).

Women	A	B (Color)
Read Some	53%	66%

This and similar tests indicate the possibility that this use of color in a department head on a spread with no other color may show good results. Further experiments along this line are now being tried.

We tried in *Wallaces Farmer* (October 5, 1957) a standard layout, black and white, in B; in A, art decorations in red. The same copy was used — the same illustration and the same head. This was designed to answer questions about art work as well as color (Figures 3.9, 3.10).

	Men A (Color)	B	Women A (Color)	B
Any This Page . .	75%	78%	53%	56%
Picture	65	56	37	42
Caption	57	61	28	42
Head	66	70	33	43
Copy Read Some .	63	73	39	49
Read Most .	55	62	29	40

In this case, as in all splits, we take a look at unchanged copy on nearby pages. If there is a difference in A and B scores on unchanged copy, especially if this copy is on the same theme as the tested copy, we make allowance for this. In this case, unchanged copy on nearby pages had A scores running 5 to 10 percentage points higher than B. Allowing for this, the B copy, without color or decorations, seemed to be making a better showing than A.

Possibly the article was too popular to make a good test. An article with a score of 40 Read Some would give more weight to the value of the color and art work.

We were hopeful about a feed ad in *Wisconsin Ag-*

riculturist (April 4, 1959). Here was functional color; the Duroc hog was entitled to be red. In A color was used on the picture, on the head and on the feed bag. Ad B was black and white (Figures 3.1, 3.2).

	Men A (Color)	B	Women A (Color)	B
Any This Ad . .	32%	33%	14%	21%
Picture	31	33	14	21
Head	20	19	4	8
Sales Copy				
Read Some . .	19	19	2	7
Read Most . .	14	10	2	2
Company name, etc.	19	16	6	6

Color was skillfully used in this ad, but apparently made no difference in the response.

Figure 3.1

Red

A

Any This Ad

Men 32%

Red Color on a Red Hog

Splashing color around on heads and decorations
hadn't done too well. More hope was attached to
"functional" use of color. This can mean a red color
on a picture of farm machinery when that farm machine habitually uses red. Or it can mean a red color
on a red Duroc hog.

We tried a split with A showing the hog in color
on a tinted background.

B was black and white.

Figure 3.2

Black

B

Any This Ad

Men 33%

Cut cash outlay for feed to
only $5.00 per hog with Murphy's

CUT YOUR FEED BILLS WITH MURPHY'S

Men's scores on the split follow. Women were less interested in hog feed. With both men and women, the color made no real difference:

	A (Color)	B (Black)
Any This Ad	32%	33%
Picture	31	33
Head	20	33
Sales Copy		
Read Some	19	19
Read Most	14	10
Company Name	19	16

Wisconsin Agriculturist, April 4, 1959

Figure 3.3

Black

A

Any This Page

Women 90%

Using Color in Heads

Repeated splits which use color heads against black have come out like the experiment on this page. The color does not seem to help or to hurt.

Here are the women's scores:

	A (Color)	B (Black)
Head	73%	77%
Read Some	81	86
Read Most	69	69

Figure 3.4

Red

B

Any This Page

Women 91%

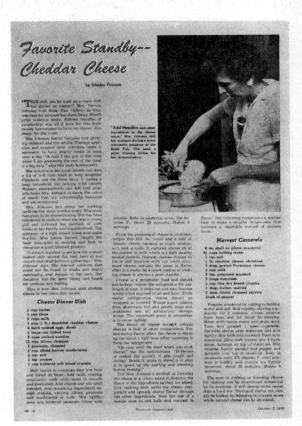

Men read very little on this page, but those who did read showed a preference for the black head (12 per cent to 4 per cent).

A few experiments using black type on a yellow background have given a slight edge to this combination as against black on white.

The over-all lesson of many splits, however, is that a head in color makes little if any difference in readership.

Wisconsin Agriculturist, October 3, 1959

12,712 lbs. of milk...
feed cost only $131.66 per cow

Figure 3.5

Red

A

Any This Ad

Men 44%

Another Split on Head Color

Farm men made up the principal audience in this split. As in similar experiments, the head in color seemed to do nothing for the page.

Men's scores:

	A (Color)	B (Black)
Picture and Head	40%	48%
Read Some	18	20
Read Most	8	14

Figure 3.6

Black

B

Any This Ad

48%

12,712 lbs. of milk...
feed cost only $131.66 per cow

Women were less interested in the ad, and the difference between A and B was slight. (Any This Ad 23 per cent for A and 16 per cent for B.)

Farmers who were milking 20 or more cows showed a slight preference for B (black).

Wisconsin Agriculturist, October 3, 1959

Figure 3.7

Red

A

Any This Ad

Women 37.2%

Reverse on Red Loses Readers

In this case, the use of a reverse head on red apparently lost readers. Scores by women follow:

	A (Color)	B (Black)
Picture	37.2%	62.0%
Head	23.3	52.0
Read Some	15.1	35.0

Figure 3.8

Black

B

Any This Ad

Women 64%

The head in black (perhaps the red circle around it gets some credit) pulled up the unchanged part of the ad for women. Men had low scores with no difference between A and B.

Women who had families of four or more gave B (black) a big Read Most vote (35.3 for B and 15.1 for A). The ad as a whole made a good showing with this important group of big families.

Wisconsin Agriculturist, November 7, 1953

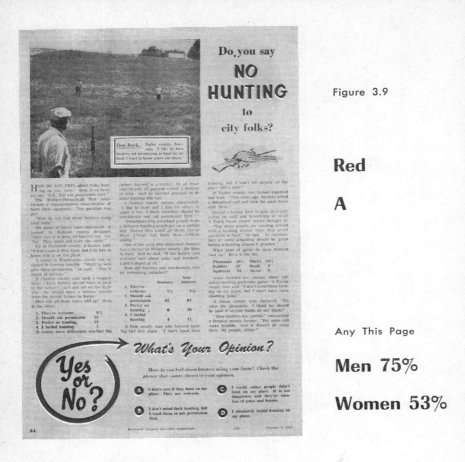

Figure 3.9

Red

A

Any This Page

Men 75%

Women 53%

Decorations and Color

This was a combination split to see if some art work in color would help the article. Here are the principal scores for men:

	A (Color)	B (Black)
Picture	65%	56%
Head	66	70
Read Some	63	73
Read Most	55	62

Figure 3.10

Black

B

Any This Page

Men 78%

Women 56%

Women gave more of an edge to B. Read Some was 39 per cent for A and 49 per cent for B.

The editors liked A better. But the readers didn't agree. There was no real difference.

Wallaces Farmer, October 5, 1957

Where does this leave us on color? We are inclined to say:

1. A head printed in color won't raise the readership score.

2. A head in reverse (white letters on color background) will not raise the score and may actually lower it.

3. A head using black overprint on color may work once in a while.

4. Color on a department head, used on a spread without other color, may do some good.

5. Decorative art work in color doesn't usually work.

6. Functional color — red hog, orange farm machinery (actual color of machine) — doesn't seem to make any difference.

7. An overprint of black type on yellow may do some good.

8. Color may pull in a few readers who are indifferent to the theme of the copy. For instance, color on a farm machinery ad may attract a few more women, but it isn't likely to make any difference with men.

9. A second color is a long shot. If used, try it on a section of the book where color is scarce.

4.

What Kind of Illustration?

IN THE EARLY DAYS of farm papers, the problem of illustration was no problem at all. Hardly any photographs or drawings were used by the editors. Advertisers relied on stiff drawings that often looked like bad wood cuts.

There have been marked changes in the use of illustrations over the years. More cuts, bigger cuts and more local farm shots are used now.

Take, for example, the third and fourth issues of March, 1930, *Wallaces Farmer* (March 15, 68 pages and March 22, 42 pages). At that time, the paper came out every week. These issues can be contrasted with the second issue in March, 1960 (March 19, 104 pages).

In 1930, we ran seven Iowa farm pictures, with a total area of 82.75 square inches or 11.82 square inches per cut. In 1960, we ran 22 Iowa farm pictures with a total of 369 square inches and an average of 16.8 square inches per cut.

These figures do not include the cover. Neither do they include pictures that did not meet the test of being taken on Iowa farms. In 1930, for instance, there was a picture page of the editor's visit to Hungary. There were also unidentified pictures of livestock and crops.

The most striking change probably is the use in 1960 of one big illustration on a page article. In 1930 and earlier, several small cuts often would be strung together.

A check of the November, 1930 and November, 1960 issues shows much the same results.

When we began readership testing, farm pictures were still enough of a novelty that almost any kind of photograph got attention. Today, the farm public is used to pictures. Many take *Look* and *Life*. Competition for attention is keener. A poor illustration isn't noticed as readily.

What makes a good illustration for a state farm paper? One farm woman gave this clue, "The first thing I do is to look through the paper and see if I know anybody in the pictures."

What she wants is a picture of somebody she can recognize. If she finds Cousin Jack Smith of Decatur County pictured in one photograph, she is pleased. If she has relatives in Calhoun County and sees a picture of some farmer, unknown to her, from that county she may say to herself, "He lives near Aunt Martha's. She probably knows him."

This local angle is pointed up by a question asked of a sample of Iowa readers by Starch in March, 1960. "Have you ever seen (in *Wallaces Farmer*) an article or a photograph about someone you know?" And 72.5 per cent said, "Yes."

How important is this local angle on photographs to advertisers? We have run tests in both Iowa and

Wisconsin to see whether readers respond better to a photograph of a home state farmer than to a photograph of an outlander.

One advertiser gives this answer, "If you have a testimonial and photograph of a farmer in Iowa, play up the address to the Iowa audience. If the photograph and testimonial belong to a farmer in Illinois, play down the address to an Iowa audience."

Our splits indicate that a local address helps a little. But, the main thing is to have the person photographed doing something that makes sense in terms of the state where the ad appears. An Illinois hog farmer, shown with his herd of hogs, will do well in Iowa. But a wheat picture from South Dakota will not impress an Iowa audience.

Another old rule still holds! Men look at pictures of men, and women look at pictures of women.

This is one reason why we like family shots when we can find a reasonable pose. Fortunately, women are around the farm frequently, and it isn't too hard to find an excuse for getting a woman into a man's picture.

How do we rank cartoons and drawings in editorial or advertising copy? Editorially, we use cartoons to slow up readers as they go through the book. But, we don't use cartoon treatment of illustrations of articles. The exception is the cartoon used on the editorial page of *Wisconsin Agriculturist* (Figure 4.12). This seems to have some value in pulling younger readers into the editorial page.

A few advertising splits using cartoons versus photographs indicate that farming is serious business. The photograph usually wins.

What about drawings? We have used sketches instead of photographs in layouts of editorial copy and each time wished we hadn't.

This is also true for ads. A photograph ordinarily outpulls a drawing. The one notable exception was a John Deere ad in *Wallaces Farmer* (September 30, 1958). Here the drawing scored 47 for men against the photograph's 39. Note, however, that the drawing used heavy lines and came closer to the weight of a photograph than the usual drawing.

Another test of photograph versus drawing came in the Starch scores in the October 17, 1959 issue of *Wallaces Farmer*. Of three page hog feed ads, one used drawings of the two farmers whose experiences were quoted. The other two used the standard photograph of the farmer quoted.

	Noted, Men	Read Most, Men
Drawing ad	20%	4%
Photograph ad (1)	36	10
Photograph ad (B)	36	11

Is one big picture better than several small ones? The answer is what you would expect. For example, a Certified Alfalfa Seed Council ad in *Wallaces Farmer* (January 16, 1960) showed one big picture versus five small ones. For men, scores were 32 for the ad with the big picture against nine for the ad with the five small pictures.

A slightly different approach was used on a cover in *Wallaces Farmer* (March 1, 1947). We played up a picture of a farm family going to the movies and accompanied it with a small picture on a different theme. In the B version, we used four pictures of equal size.

The B version did not do as well as A. Men's page score for A was 76.1 and for B, 67.7. The principal lesson however was that neither cover did especially well. Probably if we had left out the small picture in A and concentrated on one photograph — it happened to be a good one — the cover would have made more impression.

We tried a page layout illustrating the theme "How Iowa Farmers Vote" in *Wallaces Farmer* (November 4, 1950). Eight pictures were used — all about the same size — and not much text. The page score was 62.5 for men and 62 for women. It seemed clear that we would have done better to play up the most interesting photograph and to give the design a center.

Should a feed company run a picture of its president, or a picture of a hog eating its feed? Another possibility is to have the president on all fours eating the hog feed, but nobody yet has managed to get that kind of copy approved. It still happens that the ego of a company head (or the flattery of an agency) leads to the kind of copy where the principal illustration is a photo or drawing of President John K. Doe looking important.

We had a good example of this some years ago. The score for the page ad was 18.6 for men, which established some kind of record. This same company, using more rational copy in 1959, pulled 42 per cent for men on a page ad.

Does the composition of a picture help reader response? It probably does, but we have done little testing. One inadvertent test came in *Wallaces Farmer* (November 19, 1960). The cover split showed different arrangements of the same picture (Figures 4.6, 4.7).

In A was a close-up of a farmer in the hog lot, with hogs also prominent. In B was a close-up of hogs, with the farmer in background. Since the A arrangement was the conventional one, we wanted to see whether a shift away from the farmer toward the livestock would help.

Results were ambiguous. On the non-reader basis, B was better; that is, it attracted more readers. On score by readers, there was a little difference but A got the edge.

Professor Rodney Fox of the Department of Technical Journalism at Iowa State University at Ames commented:

The hogs were played up about the same in both pictures. The play given the man was the only real variable.

There may be one factor you didn't consider. In A, the man and the hogs compete for attention. The resulting tension is somewhat unpleasant.

In B, the man has been subordinated to the hogs. The resulting effect is not disturbing — in short, I think B has more pleasing composition.

It would be interesting to know how readers would have reacted had the man dominated the picture in A with the hogs subordinated to a weak background position function. And it would be interesting to know how the readers would have reacted had the hogs dominated the picture with the man even more subordinated than he is in B.

And it would be interesting to know how a non-farm audience with only the most casual interest in hogs might react.

I would have expected A to make a better showing than it did because I'm so deeply convinced of the interest of people in people. Can it be that composition is a quite important factor even in news type pictures? (1)

Editors at times mutilate a big cut by overprinting a head, cutting out a chunk to permit use of a caption, etc.

Advertisers fall into the same trap. In *Wallaces*

Farmer (November 3, 1951) Moorman ran a page ad on hog feed. In the B version, the picture filled the page, but a big area in the middle of the lower center of the cut was cut out and copy inserted. In the A version, an unmutilated three-column cut was used with sales copy running in the fourth column.

The A picture outscored the B picture with men 54 to 41. The page as a whole (Any This Ad) scored 59 for A, 42 for B.

The advertiser threw away some of the benefits of this good start, however, by putting the sales copy column on the left instead of next to the gutter and by using type that was too small on the sales copy. As a result, the Read Most scores of A and B were almost even. (2)

What value are thumbnail cuts? *Wallaces Farmer* (November 21, 1959) ran a two-column article on corn, with no illustrations, against the same article illustrated by thumbnails of four farmers quoted in the article (Figures 4.8, 4.9). Men scored like this:

	No cuts	4 cuts
Any Page	65%	82%
Read Most	54	72

This outcome wasn't difficult to predict. A tougher problem in the same issue dealt with a two-column article which started on the left-hand page, had one two-column cut and ran over in a column on the right-hand page.

It did not help to add a thumbnail to the left-hand page which already had an illustration. But, the thumbnail on the runover against no cut at all on the runover apparently helped women's readership.

The monotony of the standard two-column layout probably needs relief. We tried one way by getting more depth on the cut. In A, it was four inches deep; in B, six inches. There was no other change. This experiment in *Wallaces Farmer* (January 16, 1960) indicated a modest gain for the deeper cut (Men 60 A, 72 B).

Wisconsin experiments on whether to put the head above or below the two-column cut at the top of page also may be related to monotony. The head above the two-column cut did better than the head below. Since most of the articles used the second style, this may be a tribute to change.

On page copy, we got a somewhat different response. Here the conventional style of ads and editorial matter is to put a big cut at the top of the page. Yet an ad in *Wallaces Farmer* (September 20, 1958) gave a better score to copy at the top of page and cut at the bottom than to the reverse layout.

Another attempt to break the monotony of the standard two-column article was to set copy in 10-point, 22 picas wide, instead of two columns of 9-point each 12 picas wide. Only a slight gain for the 10-point was indicated. Yet we suspect that the change of pace may have made the book as a whole look more attractive.

"Cook's Corner," with recipes, always scores high and therefore probably needs no help. Yet we tried in *Wisconsin Agriculturist* (November 7, 1953) an A version with illustrations set into the recipes; B was all type. There was no difference in score.

For a two-column cut, should the print be trimmed

down to the principal figures or should a good deal of background be permitted? Splits on this came out as one would expect. The picture cut down to the essentials always won. A cut 24 picas wide is too small to permit much background. The same thing is more emphatically true of a 12 pica cut.

Does "What's Ahead" (the economic outlook department) need help from an illustration? *Wallaces Farmer* (January 16, 1960) found that adding the illustration made no difference. *Wisconsin Agriculturist,* in earlier tests, found the illustration helped and changed layout accordingly.

For outside comment, note the following from the Research Department, Curtis Publishing Company. (3)

"Whenever possible, it is better to use photographs rather than sketches to illustrate an article.

"Art-work illustrations seem most successful in attracting readers when they are clear and realistic, as nearly photographic in quality as possible.

"While cartoons as separate features are immensely popular, using them to illustrate a piece seems to result in lower readership than the use of the conventional photographic treatment does."

*   *   *

Our own summary (we agree with the Curtis statement above) might add these points:

1. Use pictures of farm men and farm women in working clothes occupied in farm or household chores. (Getting women to act as subjects without prettying up as if for a trip to town is a hazard for the photographer.)

2. A big picture is worth three small ones.

3. Every picture used should be identified — "This is John

Smith who farms 200 acres in Blank County, Iowa. He thinks hog prices are going down." Put the caption under the cut.

4. Farmers aren't always farming. Human interest pictures of farm families at play, on vacation, at the fair, give variety.

5. Never line up the officers of an organization in a row and take their pictures. Such photographs bring low scores.

6. Take three or four times as many good pictures as can possibly be used in the paper. Then sort for the best. (4)

Figure 4.1

Page Score

Men 86%

Women 57%

How Farm People Vote

Before every election, *Wallaces Farmer* and *Wisconsin Agriculturist* sample rural-farm townships and interview farm people. This page scored well because:

1. The theme was timely, and the election was only a few days away.
2. One big picture dominated the page.
3. Black head and black box on yellow background drew some eyes.

This survey, incidentally, indicated that Eisenhower would get 53 per cent of the farm vote in Wisconsin. In the actual tally, he got 55 per cent.

Wisconsin Agriculturist, November 3, 1956

Figure 4.2

Page Split A

Page Score

Men 47%

Women 42%

Photograph Outscores Drawing

The sketch in B pulled down the over-all page score with both men and women. Other experiments show the same results. A photograph almost always outpulls a drawing.

But notice something else. Moving the sales copy in B to the upper left, where the eye is apt to look first, made up for the damage done by the sketch.

Figure 4.3

Page Split B

Page Score

Men 28%

Women 16%

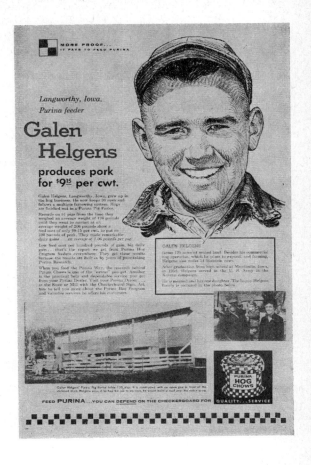

Sales Copy, Read Some	A	B
Men	11%	14%
Women	5	3

Would it pay to put the copy in the upper left, as in B, and use a photograph (as in A) elsewhere on the page?

Wallaces Farmer, January 16, 1960

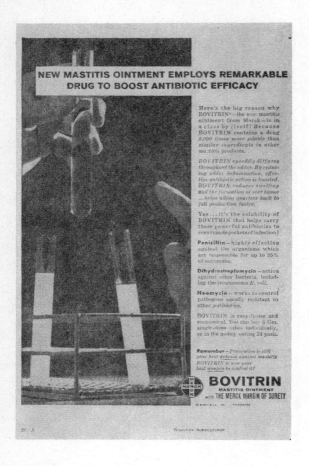

Figure 4.4

Split Page A

Ad Score

Men 20%

Women 7%

Cow Versus Test Tube

The cow won. And the superiority for B helped other parts of the ad:

		Men	
		A	B
Head		15%	28%
Picture		17	33
Sales Copy			
Read Some		11	26

Figure 4.5

Split Page B

Ad Score

Men 32%

Women 7%

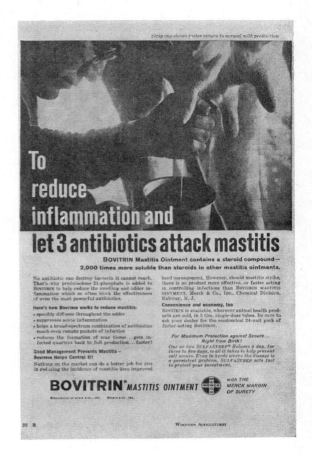

Of farmers who were having trouble with mastitis in their herds, 41.2 per cent Read Some of the B copy. Of those with NO trouble with mastitis, only 11.1 per cent Read Some of the A copy.

Of farmers with big herds (30 cows and up), 21.4 per cent Read Some of the B copy. Only 5.3 per cent had Read Some of the A copy.

Full details on this split appear in Chapter 16, pages 223–27.

Wisconsin Agriculturist, October 3, 1959

Figure 4.6

Cover Split A

Page Score

Men 97%

Women 86%

Man Versus Hogs

Sometimes farmers who are hog raisers are more interested in hogs than in people. But here we found a slight edge for the cover that played up the farmer. What would have happened if we had played up a hog in B and had left the farmer out of the photograph?

Read Some scores on sales copy also gave A (man) the advantage:

	A	B
Men	80%	73%
Women	43	36

Figure 4.7

Cover Split B

Page Score

Men 90%

Women 75%

(turn to page 16. (B))

B has one claim to superiority. There were fewer non-readers in the B group than in the A group. Perhaps the hog picture had some value here in converting possible non-readers into readers.

Both A and B scores were good. You can't lose in an Iowa farm paper by putting hogs on the cover — with or without a farmer.

Wallaces Farmer, November 19, 1960

Figure 4.8

A

No Cuts

Read Most

Men 54%

Thumbnails Help

What happens to readership when you add thumbnail cuts to a two-column story? The A version, in this split, used the standard text but with no illustrations. The B version, on the next page, inserts

[78]

Figure 4.9

This corn crop is a problem!

A lot of corn is still standing; and some may spoil in the crib

WEATHER was almost ideal for growing corn in Iowa this year—but harvesting the bumper crop is a different story.

About half the corn is still in the field. That isn't the whole story, tho—some of the corn now in the crib may be carrying too much moisture to store safely.

The cold, wet weather that has hung on in the state during the last month practically brought corn picking to a standstill.

During the second week in November, only 45 percent of the corn acres had been harvested. This compares with about 90 percent a year ago. The greatest amount of corn still standing is located in south-western and south-central Iowa.

Certainly, no one has written this wet corn off yet. But field losses will go up now as more of the corn begins to lodge and drop ears.

Seley "I decided early this fall to let my corn stand in the field until it was good and dry," says one young farmer in Van Buren county, Iowa. "Now I'm not so sure that I did the right thing."

The problems aren't limited to those folks who have corn standing in the field, tho.

Some folks did just the opposite of the Van Buren county man. They decided to go ahead and pick and store the corn even tho the high moisture content made it risky. They wanted to get it out of the field.

Warm weather in late fall could mean spoilage. Most danger to the corn cribbed too wet will come next spring, when it thaws out.

Richard Seley, Adair county, Iowa, faces this problem. But he does have a solution figured out if it's needed.

"If the moisture doesn't drop to a safe level during the winter, I'll shell the corn and dry it artificially," he says. "I decided that having the corn in the crib was better than waiting too long for some decent field drying weather."

Farmers with a livestock operation have less of a problem. High moisture corn makes excellent feed, and can be used for

that if there is a threat of spoilage present.

Niels Fuglsang, Cass county, Iowa, and son, Charles, have another option available. By spring, they'll have used up a lot of the feed now in their air-tight silo.

"If the corn isn't dry enough next spring, we can shell and store it in the silo," explains Fuglsang.

Hull

"Dryers over the state may get a good work-out this fall and next spring," says Dale Hull, extension agricultural engineer at Iowa State University. "There is a lot of corn cribbed that tests well over 20 percent moisture."

What about sealing corn? There is plenty of corn that won't meet the moisture standards. To get a government loan, the maximum content at the time of testing include: November thru February, 20½ percent; March, 19 percent; April, 17½ percent; May, 15½ percent.

If corn exceeds these limits, it can't be sealed at that time. However, it can be retested at a later date.

Corn sealed on a purchase agreement can last up to 23 percent. This corn won't be called for until late next summer, however, and some artificial drying may be necessary to prevent spoilage.

"I have a lot of ventilators in my crib that will help if I get good drying weather this winter," says Harold Van Zee, Marion county, Iowa. "The corn won't be dry enough for a government loan this fall."

Van Zee

Harvest is running behind schedule on other crops, too. There are still some fields of soybeans and grain sorghum standing in the state.

The enormous corn crop caught some folks without enough storage space, too. Corn is everywhere—in temporary cribs of snow fence, in new permanent structures, and in huge piles on the ground.

If you have corn in your crib that is a problem, it might be wise to make arrangements now for having it artificially dried.

FARMER (B) November 21, 1959

B

Thumbnails

Read Most

Men 72%

four thumbnail cuts of men mentioned in the article.

Results of the split, for men, follow:

	(No cuts) A	(Thumbnail) B
Read Some	63%	82%
Read Most	54	72

(Wallaces Farmer, Nov. 21, 1959)

Ben and Bernard Zinke's
Purina-fed herd makes...

491,698 lbs. milk
from 40 cows!!

Figure 4.10

Split Page A

Page Score

Men 61%

Women 26%

Square Cut Versus Cutout

Does it pay to cut away background on a photograph and play up the central figure?

But what is the central figure? Would it be better to play up a cow instead of the farmer?

While the picture in A outscored the cutout in B, the sales copy in B pulled up a little ahead of A.

	Men	
	A	B
Sales Copy		
Read Some	24%	27%

Figure 4.11

Split Page B

Page Score

Men 47%

Women 18%

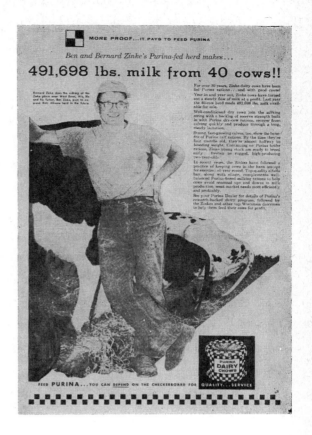

What kind of farmers read A and B? This may be more important than the total score.

Farmers with 30 cows and up:

	A	B
Read Some Sales Copy . .	31.6%	14.3%

Farmers who sold Grade A milk gave A a Read Some score twice as good (42.4 per cent to 20.8 per cent) as B.

Wisconsin Agriculturist, October 3, 1959

Figure 4.12

Split Page A

Cartoon Score

Men 46%

Women 40%

Cartoon Versus Photo

Photographs usually outscore cartoons on our papers, but not on the editorial page of *Wisconsin Agriculturist*. The cartoon shown above in A outpulled a B page in which a photograph was used in place of the cartoon.

Did the higher score for the cartoon pull up readership on the editorials? Editorials near the cartoon scored 5–10 points higher than the same editorials on the page with the photograph. Short items at the bottom of the page (farthest from the cartoon) showed less difference.

Figure 4.13

Split Page B

Photograph Score

Men 27%

Women 24%

The main value of the cartoon was in its appeal to younger readers and particularly to younger men.

	Men 21–34 years
Cartoon	75%
Photograph	24

An earlier split showed a similar advantage for the editorial page cartoon with younger readers.

Wisconsin Agriculturist, April 4, 1959

Harry E. Walsh cartoon. By permission from *How To Write Columns*, by Olin Hink and John Henry, © 1952, Iowa State University Press.

5.

Page Position and Readership

How can an editor be sure that he is holding readers throughout the magazine, from the front cover to the back? One way, of course, is to check readership surveys and see what the page scores are on each page. This is not a final answer, however, because the appeal of different articles and advertisements will vary.

Suppose that an attractive full page article on a subject of interest to the reader (possibly hogs in Iowa, dairying in Wisconsin) appears on page 13. The page scores 81 per cent for men. On page 79, there is a two-column article on sheep (not so important) with no illustration. It scores 30 per cent for men. Does this prove that readership in the back of the book is low? No, because a sheep article would score low with Iowa and Wisconsin readers in any position. A hog or dairy article would score high.

To find out whether the edtiorial matter is pulling readers through the book from front to back, use the split run. Print Article 1 on page 17 for half the run and see that it reaches half the sample of farm people interviewed. Then shift Article 1 to page 66 for the second half of the run. Get a readership score for Article 1 in each position.

In the same issue, print Article 2 on page 66 for half the run. Then shift to page 17. Get a score for Article 2 in each position.

If all the interviewers were to start from the front of the book, reader fatigue will almost automatically give the copy on page 17 a better score than the copy on page 66. What we do, therefore, in all readership surveys, is to start half the respondents in the middle of the book, go through to the last page, come back to page one and go through to the middle. The other half of the respondents are taken straight from page one to the last page. This device presumably equalizes reader fatigue. Unless this device were used, we couldn't learn much from the tests described in this chapter.

Our first test in transposing articles was in *Wallaces Farmer* (November 5, 1949). We switched two-column articles on page 12 and page 27. In each case, the article suffered when moved to page 27.

This test was repeated November 4, 1950. This time the shift was from page 12 to page 50 in a 64-page issue. We found we lost readership in the shift from page 12 to page 50. (1)

Faced by this evidence of weakness in the back of the book, the editors began to make changes. More and stronger copy was used in the back of the book. Two popular departments were given a permanent position on the inside back cover and the facing page.

We checked again in *Wallaces Farmer* (March 19, 1955). This time we switched picture pages — one on page 17 and one on 81 in an issue of 100 pages. This time page 81 lost a little but not more than the expected experimental error.

On October 1, 1955, a similar split was tried out in an 80-page issue. Two articles — each two columns in length — were transposed. Their titles were "Apply Nitrogen in Fall" and "Fertilizer Helps Stop Erosion."

Following are Read Most scores for men. The sample had 68 men and 100 women in A; 100 men and 100 women in B.

	"Apply nitrogen"		"Fertilizer helps"	
	No.	Per cent	No.	Per cent
Page 18 . . .	28	41.2%	47	47%
Page 66 . . .	25	36.8	51	51

Scores for women — much smaller — showed about the same variation.

In the 92-page March 16, 1957 issue (*Wallaces Farmer*) a similar split was tried. Again two articles — each two columns in length — were transposed. Each dealt with some aspect of cattle feeding.

Read Most scores for men on the two articles follow. The sample has 100 men and 100 women in A: the same in B. Since the sub-sample in each case is 100. the number and the percentage are the same.

	Feeder cattle	Economy supplement
	Per cent	Per cent
Page 26	46%	41%
Page 70	48	44

Later surveys were designed to see if these gains had been held. For instance, in the January 16, 1960 issue

(*Wallaces Farmer*) a corn silage article was run on page 18 in the A section and on page 60 in the B section. The "Service Bureau" was run on page 60 in A and on page 18 in B. Read Most scores for men are:

	Corn silage Per cent	Service Bureau Per cent
Page 18	29%	51%
Page 60	34	44

A shift from page 24 to page 71 showed similar results. Read Most scores for men follow:

	Good rations Per cent	Farrowing house Per cent
Page 24	17%	47%
Page 71	21	41

Women had lower scores on these articles which were aimed primarily at men. The pattern of response was the same, however.

All of these reports, except the picture page split in 1955, dealt with two-column articles. *Wisconsin Agriculturist* (April 2, 1960) tried a shift with page articles.

Here are the scores for the two pages. The switch was from page nine to page 74. The article was "How Thick Should You Plant Corn?"

	Men		Women	
	Page 9	Page 74	Page 9	Page 74
Any This Page . .	66%	59%	24%	21%
Read Some . . .	64	51	12	11
Read Most	44	36	11	6
Picture and caption	52	47	22	18

There is a slight edge for page nine, especially with the Read Most score for men. The other differences are minor.

Here are the results of another article, "The Farmer's Job in Civil Defense:"

| | Men | | Women | |
	Page 9	Page 74	Page 9	Page 74
Any This Page . .	53%	52%	39%	50%
Read Some . . .	44	51	38	49
Read Most	32	32	31	33
Maps and captions .	41	41	24	39

This comes out even, except that page 74 has the edge with women. This has happened in other splits. Apparently some women start to read with the home-making department and go on through to the back. This sometimes gives a stronger women's score in the back of the book than one might expect. The best spot for dual purpose ads or editorial matter may be in the area in back of the homemaking department.

If scores for both pages are combined, we get the following:

| | Men | | Women | |
	Page 9	Page 74	Page 9	Page 74
Any This Page .	59.9%	55.5%	31.5%	35.5%
Read Some . .	54.0	51.0	25.0	30.0
Read Most . .	38.0	34.0	21	19.5
Picture (maps) and captions . .	46.5	44.0	23	28.5

These combined scores make it clear that there is no significant difference between the two positions so far as reader interest is concerned.

The custom on *Wisconsin Agriculturist* and *Wallaces Farmer* has been to run tests like this every year to see whether readers are reading all the way through the magazine. These results are of great interest to advertisers. A good ad on page 80 presumably would have just as good a chance for readership as one in the front of the book.

Corn silage fits ration for sows

Some research indicates that silage can increase litter size

IF YOU'RE already feeding corn silage to your cattle, you may profit by feeding your sows silage, too.

"I've fed my sows silage during gestation for 3 or 4 years," says Maurice Beaver, Wapello county, Iowa. "It's easy to put some extra corn silage in the auger wagon each day."

He feeds the sows at the same time he feeds his cattle.

Sows fed properly supplemented corn silage ration produce at least as many pigs per litter as sows on more common rations. Some research even shows there can be an increase in litter size.

Other research will indicate that pigs farrowed from sows fed a corn silage ration may outdo pigs from sows fed some of the more common rations.

You'll be most apt to profit from feeding a corn silage ration if you are presently self feeding grain and supplement to your sows. With a good corn silage ration, you can cut your per sow feed cost to around 15 cents per day.

Purdue University, in a recent experiment, fed each of 10 sows 1.5 pounds of protein, plus 11.3 pounds of corn silage per day. The group averaged 9.9 pigs weaned per litter.

With protein at 6 cents per pound and corn silage at $10 per ton, the feed cost figures about 14½ cents per sow per day.

However, if you are feeding a limited ration of concentrates to your sows, you may not profit as much by changing to a corn silage ration.

Some Iowa farmers have built silos for their sow herds, but it is not a common practice. Fifty sows or more are usually required to justify a silo for your sow herd alone.

Only choice-quality silage makes good sow feed. Finely cut silage is best. Sows will sort a coarsely cut silage. And they have a strong preference for silage made from corn before it reaches the hard dent stage.

Iowa State University workers think it's best to start feeding silage 3 to 4 weeks before the sows are bred. Otherwise, don't start them on the corn silage until after breeding is over. Changing feed too close to breeding time may cut your litter size.

Feed the corn silage free-choice on a platform or in a trough. Each sow needs 8 to 10 pounds of silage.

A 20 percent protein balancer is used by Iowa State University to supplement the corn silage ration. The balancer can be made either from one of the university formulas or by mixing equal parts of shelled corn and a 30 to 35 percent protein brood sow supplement.

Feed the 20 percent balancer once each day in the following amounts:

Gifts

Flushing period .. 4 to 5 pounds
First 10 weeks
 of gestation . 3 to 3½ pounds
Last of gestation .4 to 5 pounds

Sows

Flushing period .. 4 to 5 pounds
First 10 weeks
 of gestation . 2½ to 3 pounds
Last of gestation.4 to 5 pounds

When you are starting the sows or gilts on corn silage, it's wise to add shelled corn on top of the silage to encourage them to eat it.

Corn silage is not always the same year after year. The amount of concentrate must occasionally be adjusted to the amount of corn in the silage.

Read Most

Men

Page 18, 29%

Page 60, 34%

Page 18 Versus Page 60

To see whether readership stays high all the way through the issue, articles are switched from front to back. In this case, the corn silage article ran on page 18 in the A version and on page 60 in the B version. Read Most scores are given above.

Page 60 (in an issue of 76 pages) is as good a position as page 18.

Wallaces Farmer, November 21, 1959

High Yields are possible with average planting rates when fertility is high and moisture is plentiful. George Wood, Winnebago county, has discovered 80 pats. in over 50 acres of corn.

April 5, 1969   WISCONSIN AGRICULTURE   A. 9

Figure 5.2

Corn Page

Page Scores

Page 9

Men 66%

Women 24%

Page 74

Men 59%

Women 21%

Page 9 Versus Page 74

This is another example of transposing pages in order to measure the flow of readership through the issue. In this case, the corn article appeared on page 9 of the A section and on page 74 of the B section. The defense article was on page 9 of the B section and on page 74 of the A section. This issue had a total of 84 pages.

Differences are not significant except in the case of wo-

Figure 5.3

Defense Page

Page Scores

Page 9

Men 53%

Women 39%

Page 74

Men 52%

Women 50%

men who gave the edge to page 74 on the defense article. Some women apparently start reading with the "Home" department, then go on to the back and swing around to the front of the issue again. For this reason, an article just following "Home" may do a little better with women than one in the front of the paper.

Repeated tests of this kind serve to check on the ability of the editor to keep subscribers reading from page 1 to the back cover.

Wisconsin Agriculturist, April 2, 1960

Figure 5.4

Read Most

Men

Page 71
21%

Page 24
17%

Page 24 Versus
Page 71

This is another test of the kind described in Chapter 5. Good Rations ran on page 24 in the A version of the split and on page 71 in the B version. An article on farrowing houses (not shown) was also transposed.

Adding up scores on each article in each position, we get a Read Most score of 31 per cent for men on page 71 and a Read Most of 32 per cent on page 24. In other words, an article would apparently do as well on page 71 as on page 24. This issue had a total of 88 pages.

Wallaces Farmer, January 16, 1960

Good ration can boost milk output

- **Good roughage gets most emphasis**
- **Feed grain according to production**
- **Balance ration with good protein**

TOP PRODUCTION from your dairy herd is limited by two things—the inherited ability of your cows to convert feed into milk, and the quality and quantity of that feed.

This assumes you're already providing good herd management.

There's nothing you can do right now about the inheritance of cows in your milking line. But you can make sure they are given full opportunity to yield a profitable amount of milk.

Look at it this way—it's just as bad to overfeed a poor cow as it is to be stingy with a good producer.

Iowa State extension dairyman Bob Fincham explains "only the feed left over after all other needs are met can be used by the cow to produce milk."

Underfeeding a heavy producer may not immediately show up in lowered production. A cow will temporarily rob her body of food materials to produce milk. But eventually, milk output suffers.

The Iowa State folks suggest, "A few cows adequately fed may be more profitable than any additional number that must be restricted to make feed available for the entire herd."

What are bossy's requirements before the feed she eats can be used for milk production?

● Body maintenance is the big one.

An average Holstein needs 20 pounds of hay (or hay equivalent) daily just to keep herself alive. In fact, from two-thirds to three-fourths of the roughage a cow eats is used for maintenance only.

● The developing fetus is another important user of bossy's ration.

A cow carries a calf during most of her lactation. She has to "share" her ration with this unborn calf before she can use it to produce milk. This support is especially heavy during the later stages of pregnancy when the fetus makes its most rapid growth.

● A third outlet for feed nutrients is for growth.

A heifer, calving at 24 to 26 months of age, should continue to grow for another two years or more. This additional growth is going to be vital for high lifetime production. So be sure your feeding adjusts for it.

Where do you start? Best advice is to feed liberally but not wastefully.

Current prices make good hay your cheapest source of nutrients. So pushing roughage consumption should pay off. And remember, the more roughage a cow eats, the more there is available for milk production.

Fincham suggests, "feed between 20 and 30 pounds of hay or hay equivalent daily (60 to 90 lbs. of corn silage) for each 1,000 pound cow in the herd."

"Feeding three or four times per day, rather than just once, will boost consumption," he adds.

Remember it takes only about 20 pounds of good quality legume hay to satisfy maintenance requirements of a 1,400-pound cow. But to produce 50 pounds of 4 percent milk, requirements jump approximately like this: energy, 3 times as much; protein, 4 times as much; phosphorous, 5 times as much; and calcium, 6 times as much.

Fifty to 60 pounds of hay would meet these demands. But a cow can't eat that much. Her stomach just isn't large enough. (Hay pelleting may soon remove this physical barrier.)

Here's where your home-grown grains and purchased supplements fill the gap.

"Balance your grain mixture according to the quality of the roughage you feed," advises Fincham. "Then, feed this grain according to the production of each cow."

For example, with good quality roughage, a cow producing 35 pounds of 4 percent milk needs about 8 pounds of concentrate feed. Feeding medium quality hay boosts this amount to 11 pounds.

Many dairymen use this rule of thumb: Good quality hay, 1 lb. grain per 4 lbs. milk produced; medium quality hay, 1 lb. grain per 3 lbs. milk; poor quality hay, 1 lb. grain per 2½ lbs. milk.

How about protein? With top quality hay, fed liberally, addition of your grain alone will make a balanced ration. Don't over rate your hay, tho—only leafy, sun-cured, legume forage rates top quality.

If hay is medium or low quality, you should add some protein concentrate to the grain. A 14 to 16 percent digestible protein ration is suggested for these roughages.

Vitamins and minerals are important, too. Be certain your cows are getting enough by supplementing your grain mix. And always have plenty of fresh water available.

6.

Heads That Pull in Readers

WE FOUND OUT EARLY that subject matter was more important than layout, style, illustrations or anything else. If an editor could guess what readers would be excited about at the time the paper hit the mail box and could deal with that subject, the readership score would be high.

On a head, then, the first thing is to make sure that it indicates what the copy is about. This sounds easier than it is. For one thing, it means using terms that are well-known.

One horrible example came in the Starch survey of *Wallaces Farmer* (October 15, 1960.) The poll article dealt with methods of getting cropland out of production, but the head played up the technical term "cross-compliance." One result was that the Read Most score for men was only 26 per cent, one of the lowest ever scored on a poll story.

This was an error in editorial judgment. I had thought "cross-compliance" had been talked about enough so that farmers knew what it was. I was wrong.

If the article is about hogs, get the word "hog" in the head. If it is about fertilizer, say "fertilizer." The label has value.

You want more than a label, of course. One stock head that always registers is "What Price for Hogs Next Fall?" For a human interest story, there is a wider range. "What Happened to Mary Jones" was the head of an article tracing graduates of a rural high school.

An early head about retired farmers said "To Town, to California or to Heaven." This off-beat head probably did better than a label "Retired Farmers," but we didn't try a split on it. There is danger in trying to be too bright and original at the cost of making the reader guess as to what you are talking about.

In the early years of the poll, we didn't score heads by themselves. We figured that if the Read Some score was good, that proved the head was all right. Since then, we have tried scoring heads from time to time and find once in a while that a good scoring head is not necessarily followed by a good score on the following copy. The important thing still is whether the head pulls the reader into the article. If only the head is read, it isn't much good even if it does seem to score high.

Actually I have some doubts about the accuracy of these head scores. It is harder for a respondent to remember noticing a head than to remember actually reading some of an article.

Should the head use a question or a command?

A double split was tried out in *Wisconsin Agriculturist* (November 2, 1957). Heads were as follows (Figure 6.1):

A — "New Concentrates Will Sell More Milk"

B — "Will New Concentrates Sell More Milk?"

A — "Will New Hormones Change Crops?"

B — "New Hormone Could Change Crops"

Combining the two splits for Read Some, the statement got 52 per cent with men and the question 48.5. Young men readers especially seemed to prefer the statement to the question. Women leaned slightly toward the question.

In *Wallaces Farmer* (November 5, 1949) the following heads were tested:

"Don't Plan Too Many Spring Pigs"

"Are You Planning More Pigs?"

Here the statement scored higher than the question. Apparently the readers were looking for advice, and the positive statement had more appeal.

One thing we are more sure of is this: Don't limit the size of your audience by your head. In *Wallaces Farmer* (March 4, 1944) a head, "Dairy Association Hears Report" scored 20.8 Read Some for men. "Reports Fight on Oleo" or its equivalent might have done better.

Similar disadvantages come from putting the name of a country in a head, from using "4-H" in a head or the label of any minority group. Farm Bureau, because of its large membership, can be used in Iowa.

Minority groups should not be ignored. We are entitled to use a 4-H story occasionally, a sheep story, even a bee-keeper's story. But the scores are bound to be low.

If there is any way to handle the head or copy to get the majority interested in the minority theme, use it. "These Boys Build Beef Herds" is better than "4-H Boys Build Beef Herds." On the first, you'll get the 4-H readers and some others. On the second, your audience may be limited to 4-H'ers.

Do decks (sub-titles) help a head? We have been using two lines of 18-point Bodoni and have run a number of splits to see whether this addition or others to a 36-point or 42-point head increased readership.

Here is one typical split from *Wallaces Farmer* (January 18, 1948) :

A — Head: "More Profit From Early Beef Calves" (No deck)

B — Same head as A plus deck: "Early Calves Make Better Use of Pasture; Weigh More at Market Time"

Men had 57 per cent Read Some for A and 49 per cent for B.

Another split in same issue on the same subject was:

A — Head: "Soil Insect Control"
Deck: "Deep Placement of Starter Fertilizer Calls for Shift in Soil Insecticide Application"

B — Same head, no deck

On this A had 56 per cent for Read Some for men and the same for B. Combining scores, 52.5 Read Some for men on head and deck; 56.5 for head without deck.

Apparently this kind of deck did no good. Similar

tests on other types of decks indicated the same answer. Apparently the standard two-column head does well by itself.

Some experiments with lead-ins — a short line leads into the head — indicate this way of supplementing the head may have some value.

In *Wisconsin Agriculturist* (February 18, 1956) we tried a lead-in to a one-line head "When Does It Pay To Add More Land" as against conventional two-line head and two-line deck. Read Some for men was 75 per cent for the lead-in and 65 per cent for the regular head.

Although the differences are not significant, the edge is certainly toward the lead-in.

A two-line head was run against a one-line head in *Wallaces Farmer* (November 21, 1959). The one line did a little better, 27 to 22 for Read Some with men; 57 to 49 with women.

Another test of heads came in *Wallaces Farmer* (January 18, 1959). A used the head "Collect Dividends with Farm Records" and B "Need a Fulltime Secretary Soon?" No change in type was made.

Read Some favored A with men (52 to 43) ; women favored B (32 to 26). Perhaps "secretary" pulled the women in.

Advertisers have experimented with head splits. Starcross Alfalfa in *Wallaces Farmer* (January 17, 1959), ran a big head on the left-hand page of a split in A and switched the head to the right-hand page in B. The head scored better on the left-hand page (40 to 27 for men) and Read Some on copy was also strong (23 to 10).

Allied Chemical tried a split on heads in *Wallaces Farmer* (March 17, 1956) , as follows:

A — "Crops Make Money with Arcadian"

B — "I Like Arcadian 12-12-12"

There was no significant difference, except for a slight edge to A (Read Some, men 22 to 19). Other splits indicate that "profits," "make money" etc. may sometimes be good labels for ads.

Another test of headlines was made in *Wisconsin Agriculturist* (April 5, 1958) with a fertilizer ad. Here the competition was between "Get 74 Bushel Increase from 'Tired' Cornland" and the head "Plow Down Nitrogen for Corn? Sure" (Figures 6.3, 6.4) .

On this, the second head came out better, with a score of 33 per cent against 23.2. The stronger headline pulled up copy scores. The Read Some score on sales copy was 24 for the "plow down" head and 15.9 for "74 bushel increase."

Why did farmers apparently prefer the second head? One guess is that the first head claimed too much. A 74 bushel increase may have simply looked too big. A Wisconsin farmer who averaged 50 bushels might add the 74 to 50, whistle and say, "It can't be done."

The second head, incidentally, scored where it counted, among larger corn growers and among those who said they used nitrogen on corn.

Wisconsin Agriculturist, working with Herman Felstenhausen of the Department of Agricultural Journalism, University of Wisconsin, checked the influence of using the profit motive in the head. In the issue of April 2, 1960, in eight splits, one head played up profits and the other head workmanship, interest in conservation or some other non-profit motive (Figure 6.4). Here are two examples. The scores are the percentage of men readers of the issue who read some or most of the article:

Build Corn Profit **With Weed Killers** 46%	**vs.**	**Keep Corn Clean** **With Weed Killers** 52%
Build Better Herd **With DHIA Testing** 54%	**vs**	**Boost Herd Income** **With DHIA Testing** 46%

When all the results were considered, Felstenhausen concluded, "The results showed no preference for one motivation headline over another." (1)

You can put "dollars" in the headline, but it may not work. Heads stressing conservation, the pleasure of doing a good job or other motives may get just as good a response.

It seems plain that a good deal more work should be done with heads. In case after case, we find instances where a good head has pulled up a mediocre story; a poor head has lowered the score on a good story.

* * *

What should a good head have?

1. The good head should have plenty of white space around it. The jammed up head suffers.

2. The old two-line deck doesn't seem to have much value. Try more lead-ins.

3. Put a label on the story. Is it about hogs, or dairy cattle, or fertilizer, or what? Sometimes this can be handled as a lead-in.

4. After labelling the story, try to get some color into the rest of the head. Quotes can have value.

5. Perhaps it would pay to have the writer of an article submit four or five heads. Let the desk try to work up a few more. Sort for the best.

6. Don't use words that the reader can't understand. Technical language, in ads or editorial copy, will not get across.

7. If you want to attract a minority group — tobacco growers, honey producers, maple sugar makers — a head so labelled is useful in pulling in these particular folks. But it may repel the rest of your audience. Playing to minorities makes sense at times, but know what you are likely to gain and what you are likely to lose.

Figure 6.1

Question Head

Read Some

Men 53%

Women 16%

RIST AND FARMER   November 2, 1957

Gibberellic Acid caused corn at right to grow faster and tassle slightly earlier than corn at left. At harvest time, there was no difference in height or yield, however.

Will New Hormone Change Crops?

GIBBERELLIC acid promises to be an important tool for farmers, truck gardeners, fruit and flower growers.
S. H. Wittwer of Michigan State University, where much work with gibberellic acid has been done, says the new chemical has six promising possibilities.
1. Producing earlier maturity in some crops.
2. Speeding up the flowering of such annuals as lettuce and radishes for seed production.
3. Hastening the germination of

earlier in the spring. Bluegrass and Bermuda grass begin growing earlier and faster. Brown summer-dormant bluegrass greens up after spraying.
In greenhouse tests bush snapbeans and shell-beans flowered two to three days earlier, set more pods and had mature seed a week earlier when they were treated. Treated broccoli developed marketable heads 10 to 15 days earlier.

Results May Vary

Question vs. Statement

The only change in the articles reprinted here is the shift from question to statement in the head. A second split on "Keeping Corn Clean" also showed little difference in response to the two kinds of heads.

An earlier split on "Planning More Spring Pigs" gave the edge to the statement in preference to the question. Sometimes folks want positive advice.

Wisconsin Agriculturist, November 2, 1957

Statement Head

Read Some

Men 50%

Women 14%

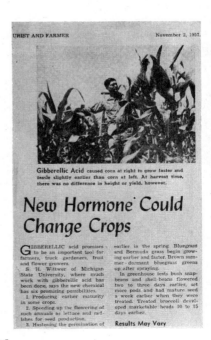

URIST AND FARMER   November 2, 1957.

Gibberellic Acid caused corn at right to grow faster and tassle slightly earlier than corn at left. At harvest time, there was no difference in height or yield, however.

New Hormone Could Change Crops

GIBBERELLIC acid promises to be an important tool for farmers, truck gardeners, fruit and flower growers.
S. H. Wittwer of Michigan State University, where much work with gibberellic acid has been done, says the new chemical has six promising possibilities.
1. Producing earlier maturity in some crops.
2. Speeding up the flowering of such annuals as lettuce and radishes for seed production.
3. Hastening the germination of

earlier in the spring. Bluegrass and Bermuda grass begin growing earlier and faster. Brown summer-dormant bluegrass greens up after spraying.
In greenhouse tests bush snapbeans and shell-beans flowered two to three days earlier, set more pods and had mature seed a week earlier when they were treated. Treated broccoli developed marketable heads 10 to 15 days earlier.

Results May Vary

From 50 bu. per acre to 124 bu. per acre is quite a jump in corn yields, yet that's the amazing increase Wayne Fix, left, got on his St. Charles, Minn., farm.

Gets 74 Bushel Increase from "Tired" Cornland

Read how Wayne Fix used a plow-down of Spencer "Mr. N" Ammonium Nitrate plus starter fertilizer to increase his corn yields from 50 bu. per acre to 124 bu. per acre

Figure 6.2

Split Page A

Page Score

Men 32.9%

Women 21.6%

Strong Head Helped This Ad

Only one change was made in this split. The head in A read "Gets 70 Bushel Increase from 'Tired' Cornland." The head in B read "Plow-Down Nitrogen For Corn? Sure!"

The B head had the higher score and pulled up the rest of the B ad with it.

	Men	
	A	B
Head	20.7%	33%
Sales Copy		
Read Some	15.9	24

Figure 6.3

Split Page B

Page Score

Men 49%

Women 26%

Farmers who used nitrogen on corn gave B the advantage.

Men

Any This Ad	Use nitrogen on corn	Don't use
A	22.7%	25.0%
B	34.0	30.0

Farmers with larger corn acreages also preferred B — as did farmers who generally used some kind of commercial fertilizer.

Why did the B head win? One possibility is that A claimed too much. A farmer, who habitually got 50 bushels of corn to the acre, might be dubious about the possibility of increasing the yield 70 bushels, up to a total of 120 bushels.

Wisconsin Agriculturist, April 5, 1958

Figure 6.4

Heads

Read Some

"Corn clean"

Men 52%

Profit

vs. Workmanship

Does it increase readership to put dollars in the head — such as, "Build Corn Profit with Weed Killers" instead of "Keep Corn Clean with Weed Killers" or "Boost Herd Income" instead of "Build Better Herd."

Farmers don't always respond to the profit theme. A series of splits found that putting "dollars" or "profit" in the head was not a sure way to high scores.

Wisconsin Agriculturist, April 2, 1960

Read Some

"Corn profit"

Men 46%

Keep Corn Clean with Weed Killers

JUST how good are those new chemicals for weed control in corn?

Chemicals—simazine and atrazine—have produced some startling results. They've also caused disappointment.

The decision whether or not to use them this spring will need to be made soon. Pre-emergence weed killers should be applied at corn planting time. They don't work effectively after weeds come up.

There's no doubt that the chemicals provide a major breakthrough in corn weed control—if conditions are right for their use. But under the wrong conditions they can be an expensive mistake.

Cost Is High

Your choice between the two—simazine and atrazine—is nearly a tossup. So says Kenneth Buchholtz, University of Wisconsin agronomist. Simazine has been on the market three years. Atrazine came out last year. Atrazine appears a little better in research to date.

Their main drawback so far is cost.

The spraying should be done at planting time or within the next three days. Early application increases the chances of getting ahead of spring rains.

Equip your sprayer with 20-gallon nozzles and coarse nozzle screens to prevent clogging. Be sure the sprayer has an agitator or a large pump that returns part of the flow to the tank. This constant mixing assures even spray distribution.

Avoid excessive over-dosage. Heavy application may leave a residue which could affect grain crops the following year. Oats are especially sensitive.

If grassy weeds are not a serious problem and if the corn field is well drained, then you can turn to other weed control measures.

After broad leaf weeds come up, 2,4-D works well. Apply it before the corn is 10 inches tall. Later treatment may damage the corn unless drop nozzles are used to keep the spray off the corn leaves.

Perennial weeds require special treatment. Don't neglect them in planning your weed control pro-

Build Corn Profit with Weed Killers

JUST how good are those new chemicals for weed control in corn?

Chemicals—simazine and atrazine—have produced some startling results. They've also caused disappointment.

The decision whether or not to use them this spring will need to be made soon. Pre-emergence weed killers should be applied at corn planting time. They don't work effectively after weeds come up.

There's no doubt that the chemicals provide a major breakthrough in corn weed control—if conditions are right for their use. But under the wrong conditions they can be an expensive mistake.

Cost Is High

Your choice between the two—simazine and atrazine—is nearly a tossup. So says Kenneth Buchholtz, University of Wisconsin agronomist. Simazine has been on the market three years. Atrazine came out last year. Atrazine appears a little better in research to date.

Their main drawback so far is cost.

The spraying should be done at planting time or within the next three days. Early application increases the chances of getting ahead of spring rains.

Equip your sprayer with 20-gallon nozzles and coarse nozzle screens to prevent clogging. Be sure the sprayer has an agitator or a large pump that returns part of the flow to the tank. This constant mixing assures even spray distribution.

Avoid excessive over-dosage. Heavy application may leave a residue which could affect grain crops the following year. Oats are especially sensitive.

If grassy weeds are not a serious problem and if the corn field is well drained, then you can turn to other weed control measures.

After broad leaf weeds come up, 2,4-D works well. Apply it before the corn is 10 inches tall. Later treatment may damage the corn unless drop nozzles are used to keep the spray off the corn leaves.

Perennial weeds require special treatment. Don't neglect them in planning your weed control pro-

7.

More Experiments in Readership

WHAT GOOD has this testing done the two papers? If you put readership scores on a long chart, you find a lot of zig-zags but no impressive gains over the years. Like another famous character, by running as fast as we could, we have managed to stay in the same place.

For a brief illustration, look at the readership scores for *Wallaces Farmer* in March 9, 1940 and January 16, 1960.

How many non-readers then and now?

										Men	Women
1940	.	.	.	.	.	.	.	.	.	23%	20.7%
1960	.	.	.	.	.	.	.	.	.	18	24.5

A look at the 20 year report on non-readers indicates a little change. Allow for bad weather, rush seasons, etc., and you come out in about the same place.

What about readership scores? Another small sample shows.

Lead editorial	Read Most — Men
1940 "Sell More Lard"	53.3%
1960 "What Do Price Supports Do"	54.5

"Country Air," for women, in 1960 scored within a few points of the 1940 figure. Copy on hogs ran a little higher in 1960.

If you look at the long chart, it seems that the war period brought an increase in readership. It brought more important news on farm programs, ceilings, etc. There was also less chance to get away from home on account of gas rationing.

Crises bring more readership. We don't know what the AAA period in the 'thirties would have scored since we didn't survey then. A guess is that scores would have been high. When everything is going smoothly, readership drops. When there is an early frost, a drop in the price of hogs or a new farm program, readership picks up.

It should be remembered that since 1940, television has come into its own. Farmers are getting more magazines. The competition for attention is greater. Perhaps it is something for a farm paper to have held its own.

We guess that reading habits have changed even though scores have not. Today, for instance, we are fairly sure that a good many readers pick up the paper for a few minutes, lay it down, then pick it up again later. The ideal reader who settles down in his chair and reads the paper for two hours is getting scarcer.

Actually we have no early figures on this, because we

didn't start asking this question until a few years ago. But in *Wallaces Farmer* (October 18, 1958), Starch found this:

Less than one-half hour	19.5%
One-half hour to less than 1 hour	26.0
One hour	19.5
One to less than 2	15.0
Two to less than 3	14.0
Three hours or more	5.5
Not stated	0.5

Another change probably has come in what is called "reading days." If you pick up the paper to read it on Monday, that's one day; if you repeat on Tuesday, that gives you two days, etc. We have checked this and find the average is close to three reading days.

If you look at a 1940 issue, you may be inclined to say that 1960 issues look more readable. For one thing, type is larger.

When we began our surveys in Iowa we were using 8-point Bodoni on a 9-point slug for narrow measure copy — 12½ picas — and 10-point on a 12-point slug for full page, 17 pica columns.

We have stayed by 10 on 12 for the full page copy or for any place where we can use a wide line — 17 to 22 picas. On narrow measure, however, we have moved up to 9 on 11.

The face has changed. In Iowa we shifted from Bodoni to Paragon for body type, but found it a little weak. A heavier, blacker face seemed desirable. Experiments by other people confirmed this view. So we moved over to Corona; wide measure, 10 on 12; narrow. 9 on 11.

Wisconsin Agriculturist moved to Excelsior with 8 on 10 for narrow measure, 10 on 12 for wide, and recently shifted to Times Roman with 10-point for narrow and 12-point for wide measure.

Why are we using larger type? The Minnesota Poll (*Minneapolis Tribune*) reports that of its readers, seven out of 10 adults wear eyeglasses. In our Iowa sample, 62 per cent wear glasses. Some of these glasses, moreover, may be the dime store variety. Lighting is bad in some farm homes. Thus, it seems that large, clear type has an advantage.

For the most part, we have taken the word of other experimenters in this field. We ran one split in Wisconsin which threw some light on the use of leading.

On the editorial page, we ran one version in 10-point solid and the other in 8-point on a 10-point slug. It was interesting to note that several people said, "Why test the obvious? Of course the bigger type will get more readers."

It didn't. The extra leading made up for the difference in type size. The 8-point came out a little better than the 10-point.

As noted elsewhere, we have run wide (22 picas) 10-point against narrow (12 picas) 9-point and couldn't find much difference. In a slightly different split, however, we ran 10-point (16½ picas) against 9-point (12 picas) in a half-page space (Figure 7.1).

In this split in *Wallaces Farmer* (January 16, 1960) women came out even but men scored as follows:

	A (wide 10-point)	B (narrow 9-point)
Read Some	54%	50%
Read Most	50	41

An unchanged ad on the same page gave an edge to A (32 to 26) but the Read Some on the sales copy was in B's favor — 13 to 17. A breakdown by age on the article showed more difference:

	A (wide 10-point)	B (narrow 9-point)
Men of 50 and up . .	**62.2%**	**41.9%**

The size of the sub-sample was 37 for A and 43 for B.

Women, 50 and over, showed the same preference for larger type. There was a similar approval from women who had only been to school from one to eight years.

We are inclined to think that the larger type (with plenty of white space) may be a help to older people. It is possible that younger folks, educated to big type in magazines, may also show the same preference. It would take more experiments, however, to be sure of this.

*   *   *

One continual argument on the staff is about the way dirt copy is to be handled. Is it enough to say, "Do this and that for your hogs," quote experiment station results and stop?

Or should we go in the field, interview several farmers, quote them and then add experiment station results?

The second method costs more. Presumably it makes the reader feel that the paper is thinking in terms of farm people like himself. But is it worth the expense and trouble?

This is a vital issue, but a hard thing to test. As

noted in the chapter on illustrations, it seems that readers do look for pictures and quotes of people they know. But this may be a long time effect. Measuring one article, written in different ways, may not be enough.

We have attempted this experiment several times. *Wisconsin Agriculturist* in splits has not been able to find that the farm visit and quote method pulled in any more readers than the desk copy.

Wallaces Farmer tried a split (September 20, 1958) with personalized dirt copy against desk copy with a few quotes and had somewhat different results.

Heads and leads of the two versions follow:

A—(Head)   "I got my bellyfull of the stuff."
             So says one Iowa farmer. But grain sorghum still looks like a good crop.

  (Lead)   "I swore last fall that I'd never raise grain sorghum again," said . . .

B—(Head)   Harvest sorghum early.
             Better count on using a crop dryer too.
             Sorghum lodges easily soon after frost.

  (Lead)   Combine your grain sorghum early and dry it, etc.

In the body of the article A, a few personal touches were added to the description of the men interviewed. A quoted two farmers not quoted in B. A had 46 lines of quotes; B had 27 lines of quotes.

It should be noted that B wasn't pure desk copy. Interviews were used, but not to the same extent as in A.

Men		A	B
Read Some	. . . . . .	54%	27%
Read Most	. . . . . .	47	22

Women also had a two to one margin ratio for A.

Sorghum raisers presumably would be more interested than non-raisers. A had 66.7 per cent Read Most
for raisers against 50 per cent for B. For non-raisers, A
had 44 per cent and B 13.7 per cent.

As usual, the frills counted more with readers who
were not greatly interested. Sorghum raisers were apparently ready to read the article whether or not it had
quotes and people.

Space is a problem here, of course. It takes more
room to get in these personal descriptions, colorful
quotes, etc. Yet the local angle and the personal angle
are important. But to work these angles takes staff, expense money and time.

* * *

One series of experiments dealt with the use of
boxes — whether to put a rule around a box or let
white space set it off. For example, a box on corn
supply with an article on the same theme, *Wallaces
Farmer* (November 5, 1949) used a sample of 98 men
in A and 97 in B.

Box — Men	A (Rule) No.		B (No rule) No.	
Read Some	22	22.4%	41	42.3%
Read Most	22	22.4	40	41.2

The unchanged article copy gave B a 4.5 point advantage on Read Most. The changed box gave B (no
rule) an advantage of 18.8 points. Allowing for this
4.5 shift in scores on unchanged A and B copy, we have
a net advantage of 14.3 percentage points for the box
without the rule (Figures 7.2, 7.3).

This was a characteristic response, where the box

was closely related to the article and was run at the bottom of the page. We found, however, that when the box was blown up to a large size with a cut it took on the nature of a separate article and the rule made no difference.

Later tests in *Wisconsin Agriculturist* indicated that a box above the head on a two-column article scored equally well with or without the rule.

White space is probably as good as a rule and sometimes better since the rule may check the movement of the eye. However the unexpected result of the series of tests was something else.

We kept finding out that the box, no matter how handled, usually scored lower than the copy it accompanied and always lower than a good photograph. For example, in *Wallaces Farmer* (March 16, 1957) the article in A scored 67 Read Most while the boxed chart (more dramatic than the usual box) scored 47 Read Most. In B the article scored 69 Read Most and the boxed chart 44 Read Most. The box, with or without the rule, was no great help to the article. A photograph would have done much more.

Another experiment in *Wisconsin Agriculturist* (November 5, 1955) had the same moral. There was a men's score of 80 per cent on the copy and a score of 56 per cent on the box. Stated in another way, of the 129 men who read some of the copy, only 87 also looked at the box.

This was a high scoring article (on Secretary of Agriculture Ezra Benson and his policies), and the box may have suffered on this account. Yet the purpose of the box is to stop the straying eye and coax it into the copy. This didn't happen.

Our tentative conclusion, therefore, is that the box, in any form, isn't likely to do what it is supposed to do; namely, draw attention to itself and the article. Putting a rule around the box — if at the bottom of the page — probably hurts it.

Today, we rarely use boxes except in the case of poll articles where the results are summarized. We even have some doubts about this.

*   *   *

Is it worth while running a table of contents near the front of the magazine? *Wallaces Farmer* tried to check on this (March 16, 1957).

The A section ran an article; the B ran a table of contents. Both were two columns (Figure 7.4).

More people read the article than looked at Contents. (Read Some, 65 to 50 for men; 56 to 27 for women). But did Contents help the articles it plugged?

Seventeen plugged articles — Read Some — were matched with 17 non-plugged articles.

Where the articles were not plugged in either A or B, the A sample had an advantage of 14.1 percentage points. Apparently the A and B samples were not well-matched in this experiment. The plugged articles in A had only an 11.5 percentage point advantage over the unplugged articles in B. The corrected difference was 2.6 points. As far as this experiment shows, the plugs in the Table of Contents did not help the respective articles.

Other experiments with plugs on the cover show much the same thing. The cover plug may help to pull the respondent into the magazine; it apparently does not help the score of the particular article plugged.

There is one big exception to this. When the cover

picture, the head and the caption are linked together to plug one article inside, there is evidence that the plugged article does gain.

* * *

A curious (to an editor) complaint comes up once in a while. An advertiser may say that editorial copy is too interesting; it diverts attention from the advertising.

Actually any advertiser wants an interesting magazine. Otherwise he'd have no readers. But an advertiser on page 31 may think that pages one to 29 and pages 32 to 100 should be exciting. Only the editorial copy on page 30, facing his ad on page 31, should be dull. (1)

To any editor, this seems nonsense. But the notion pops up once in a while. Roy Eastman in *Printers' Ink* (1951) said, "When you get your ad next to particularly absorbing 'reading matter' you just buy yourself a handicap, for even your 'visibility' is decreased."

It doesn't work that way for a state farm paper. We used a split on this. Scores are Read Most for editorial copy and Any This Ad for the ad. Men's scores are:

Copy A 30%	Ad C	20%
Copy B 51	Ad C	32

Now Ad C was the same in each case; only the editorial matter was changed. The editorial copy in B happened to be more interesting than that in A. The more interesting editorial copy pulled up the ad scores.

We ran seven splits of this kind, with scores for both men and women. Since the copy in each case was aimed at men, the men's scores were higher and the results probably more useful.

Of the seven men splits, an increase in the score of the editorial matter facing the ad was accompanied by an increase in the score of the ad in five cases. In two cases, a slight increase in the editorial score was accompanied by a drop in the ad score.

With women, the result was the same — five out of seven.

So far as we can tell, therefore, the chances are that an interesting article will help the ad next to it. (2)

My own hunch is that Eastman may have been thinking of fiction running from one page to the next. If a reader got bound up in the fortunes of Jack and Jill, he might overlook the accompanying ad. However, when no article is carried beyond the spread on which it starts, a reader must lift his eyes and the ad, if attractive, has a chance.

Bigger Type for Old Folks

The articles on the next page are the same except for type size and column width. The upper article is set in 9-point Corona on an 11-point slug and the columns are 12½ picas wide. The lower article is set in 10-point Corona on 12, 16½ picas wide.

For men, the bigger type seemed to help readership. It apparently made little difference with women.

Age break-downs for men showed a considerable edge for the larger type with older men.

Read Most	Wide, 10-point	Narrow, 9-point
Men of 50 and up . .	**62.2%**	**41.9%**

A number of splits in this field give a slight but not decisive margin to somewhat larger type.

Wallaces Farmer, January 16, 1960

Figure 7.1

Read Most

9-point type

Men 41%

Read Most

10-point type

Men 50%

Figure 7.2

Copy Split A

Read Some, Box

Men 22.4%

Rule Versus White Space

If you run a box with an article, do you put a rule around the text or let white space divide the box from the rest of the copy?

A series of experiments indicates that on copy like that in Figure 7.2 and Figure 7.3, white space does better than a rule.

IOWA HOMESTEAD
November 5, 1949

Washington Wire

Will New Farm Law Help You?

Your Share — If You Raise Corn, If You Milk Cows, Or If You Raise Hogs

WASHINGTON, D. C. — Every farmer wants to know — right now — what the new farm law will do for the price of things he sells in 1950. Here are some of the answers.

CORN GROWER: The new parity is $1.46 per bushel, as compared with the present parity of $1.55. Under the act, you take whichever is higher. That means the corn loan next year will be about the same as this year.

HOG RAISER: New parity is $10 per hundred. Sounds good? Yes, but wait. The secretary of agriculture can support hog prices at any point between 0 and 90 per cent of parity. Which point will he choose?

Suppose he picks 90 per cent of parity. That means he'll have to buy a lot of pork to support the price. Then what does he do with the pork?

He can give it away to schools for lunches, to charitable institutions, or he can trade it abroad — at a loss — for goods we need. That will take a lot of money.

One estimate — a low one — says hogs will add up to 105 million dollars for two years. It could cost a lot more.

So the hog raiser doesn't know what kind of supports he'll get. Not yet, anyway.

DAIRYMAN: The new law directs the secretary of agriculture to support dairy products at 75 to 90 per cent of parity. The new parity is $4.41 per hundred for whole milk, 70 cents per pound for butterfat. How does he do it? He buys cheese, butter, dried milk, and stores them.

Then what happens? As with pork, he can give them away to schools for lunches, charitable institutions, or dump abroad. As long as the money holds out.

What happens to egg prices? Parity drops to 45 cents. But the secretary may support the price at anywhere from 0 to 90 per cent.

Where does he put supports? It depends on how many dried eggs he has to buy to keep up the price, how many dried eggs he can sell, and how much money he is allowed to spend.

For wheat and cotton and tobacco — like corn — the future is clear enough next year. You get 90 per cent of parity on loans. And you stick to your allotments — or to your marketing quotas.

Will corn have acreage allotments in 1950? Yes. How much will the cut be? Talk is about a 15 per cent cut, but we'll know for sure in a few weeks.

Will corn farmers vote on marketing quotas? Maybe. Corn supplies are right on the line. The secretary could find good reason for ordering an election on quotas — or for avoiding an election.

If marketing quotas come up to a farm election the livestock man will face this prospect:

If quotas come and if he doesn't cut corn acreage he'll have to lock up on the farm the corn grown on the surplus acres. He can't feed or sell that corn without paying a penalty per bushel equal to half the parity price.

How will the Department of Agriculture administer the new

You Never Had

So Much Old Corn

If you're like the average U. S. corn farmer, you have on hand more old corn than ever before. Even more than in 1940.

Look at the record of old corn carried over on October 1 of various years:

Year	Bushels Carry-Over
1933	386,000,000
1937	65,000,000
1938	362,000,000
1940	644,000,000
1946	173,000,000
1948	125,000,000
1949	815,000,000

It took from 1937 to 1940 to increase the corn supply by 600 million bushels. But it only took one year — from 1948 to 1949 — to increase the supply by 700 million.

With another record crop this year, what will corn carry-over look like in 1950? And where will we put it?

Washington Wire

Will New Farm Law Help You?

Your Share — If You Raise Corn, If You Milk Cows, Or If You Raise Hogs

WASHINGTON, D. C. — Every farmer wants to know—right away—what the new farm law will do for the prices of things he sells in 1950. Here are some of the answers:

CORN GROWER: The new parity is $1.47 per bushel, as compared with the present parity of $1.55. Under the act, you take whichever is higher. That means the corn loan next year will be about the same as this year.

HOG RAISER: New parity is $19 per hundred. Sounds good? Yes, but wait. The secretary of agriculture can support hog prices at any point between 0 and 90 per cent of parity. Which point will he choose?

Suppose he picks 90 per cent of parity. That means he'll have to buy a lot of pork to support the market. Then what does he do with the pork?

He can give it away to schools for lunches, to charitable institutions, or he can trade it abroad—at a loss—for goods we need. That will take a lot of money.

One estimate—a low one—says loss will add up to 169 million dollars for two years. It could cost a lot more.

So the hog raiser doesn't know what kind of supports he'll get. Not yet, anyway.

DAIRYMAN: The new law directs the secretary of agriculture to support dairy products at 75 to 90 per cent of parity. The new parity is $4.41 per hundred for whole milk, 70 cents per pound for butterfat. How does he do it? He buys cheese, butter, dried milk, and stores them.

Then what happens? As with pork, he can give them away to schools for lunches, charitable institutions, or dump abroad. As long as the money holds out.

What happens to egg prices? Parity drops to 49 cents. But the secretary may support the price at anywhere from 0 to 90 per cent.

Where does he put supports? It depends on how many dried eggs he has to buy to keep up the price, how many dried eggs he can sell, and how much money he is allowed to spend.

For wheat and cotton and tobacco — like corn — the future is clear enough next year. You get 90 per cent of parity on loans. And you stick to your allotments—or to your marketing quotas.

Will corn have acreage allotments in 1950? Yes. How much will the cut be? Talk is about a 15 per cent cut, but we'll know for sure in a few weeks.

Will corn farmers vote on marketing quotas? Maybe. Corn supplies are right on the line. The secretary could find good reasons for ordering an election on quotas —or for avoiding an election.

If marketing quotas come up to a farm election, the livestock man will face this prospect:

If quotas carry, and it he doesn't cut corn acreage, he'll have to look up on the farm the corn grown on the surplus acres. He can't feed or sell that corn without paying a penalty per bushel equal to half the parity price.

How will the Department of Agriculture administer the new

*   *   *   *   *   *

You Never Had

So Much Old Corn

If you're like the average U. S. corn farmer, you have on hand more old corn than ever before. Even more than in 1940.

Look at the record of old corn carried over on October 1 of various years:

Year	Bushels Carry-Over
1933	386,000,000
1937	65,000,000
1938	362,000,000
1940	644,000,000
1946	173,000,000
1948	125,000,000
1949	815,000,000

It took from 1937 to 1940 to increase the corn supply by 600 million bushels. But it only took one year—from 1948 to 1949—to increase the supply by 700 million.

With another record crop this year, what will corn carry-over look like in 1950? And where will we put it?

Figure 7.3

Copy Split B

Read Some, Box

Men 42.3%

On other types of box, there seems little difference between the rule and no rule.

Most important is the fact that in almost all of the splits, the box, no matter how treated, scored lower than the accompanying article. A photograph apparently did more to get readers for the article than a box.

Wallaces Farmer, November 5, 1949

[121]

Figure 7.4

Read Some

Men 50%

Women 27%

Does a Table of Contents Help Readership?

In this split, B carried a Table of Contents and A ran an article on school reorganization. The article got more readers than the Table of Contents.

Read Some	Contents	Article
Men . . .	50%	65%
Women . .	27	56

More important than the score is this question: Did the plugged articles in Contents do better than the unplugged articles? The answer is: No real difference.

Wallaces Farmer, March 16, 1957

In this Issue

March 16, 1957

New Features

Livestock

Marketing and Management

Crops and Machinery

For Everybody

For the Home

Old Friends

IOWA HOMESTEAD   (B)   March 16, 1957

What do we think we have found out in the experiments reported in this chapter? Here are some tentative conclusions:

1. It pays to check back once in a while and see if your articles on a particular subject are scoring as well as they did last year, five years ago and 10 years ago. Don't feel too badly if you haven't gained. Competition is getting tougher. If you fall short in any particular area, start finding out why.

2. It costs more to interview and photograph many farm people in building up experience articles. We think it pays, but it is hard to get adequate evidence.

3. Personalized copy — details about Jim Smith — probably goes over a little better than copy without quotes and case histories. But, remember that the hero of every article should be the reader; he should say, "This fits my case."

4. Putting a rule around a box sometimes hurts and sometimes makes no difference. The important point here is that a box almost never scores as high as a photograph. To break up a page, a photograph makes more sense than a box.

5. An advertisement that runs next to a good article is likely to benefit. But when readership is high and continuous throughout the magazine, an ad anyplace will get readership in accordance with its merits.

8.

What Kind of Folks
Read Your Ad or Article?

SUPPOSE AN ADVERTISEMENT for hog feed finds 80 readers out of a sample of 200. That looks like a good score.

But also suppose that 60 of these readers aren't raising hogs. That leaves only 20 readers who are the kind of prospects the advertiser wants to reach.

This happens more often than you might think. A flashy photograph may pull in some casual readers. It may not pull in and hold the prospects the advertiser wants.

To measure the effectiveness of an ad we need to know more than just how many folks noticed it and how many read the sales copy. We also need to know what kind of folks did the noticing and the reading.

Wallaces Farmer and *Wisconsin Agriculturist* call this kind of investigation "market analysis." It is probably the most helpful thing a farm paper can do for its advertisers.

The same kind of "market analysis" is also useful with articles prepared by the editors. Did an article prepared for young renters really reach them? Did an article aimed at women with big families get read by that kind of subscriber?

Starting in 1951, we prepared market analyses of this kind on a number of articles and ads. In many cases, the analysis showed the ad to be stronger or weaker than you would guess from the score of the whole sample.

For instance, how well did an ad aimed at cattle feeders reach its mark? (Schering Corporation — Trilafon — September 20, 1958, *Wallaces Farmer*).

The ad scored 26.5 per cent with men. That is, 53 men out of the 200 in the sample looked at the ad. But what kind of folks were these 53?

The Poll asked whether farmers were feeding or planning to feed cattle. Here is the response:

Any This Ad	No. of interviews	No. of ad readers	Per cent
Plan to feed	82	29	35.3%
Do not plan to feed . . .	105	23	21.9
Undecided about feeding	9	1	11.1

This ad reached a fair share of the possible prospects.

An Oliver ad for field shelling of corn in *Wallaces Farmer* (September 20, 1958) needed to define its prospects in a little different way. The Poll asked:

"What do you think about the future of field shelling corn?"

"1) I'm doing it or thinking seriously about doing it.

"2) Looks interesting, but don't know whether it will work well.

"3) It isn't practical."

The three groups scored as follows:

	No. of interviews	No. of "Any This Ad" readers	Per cent of ad readers
1. Convinced	26	8	30.8%
2. On the fence	120	47	39.2
3. Opposed	44	22	50.0

Note that the men who said, "It isn't practical" were still the best readers. For the long pull, the ad's major service may have been to shake the convictions of this hostile group.

Another way to check on this ad was by corn acres. In this case, the farmers with 75 acres or more in corn had a 43.4 per cent score. This was the largest group, in terms of acres, and the ad scored better with these folks than with smaller farmers.

How does this method work with articles by the editors? Take the department "What's Ahead," a discussion of market prospects. In the same issue of *Wallaces Farmer* (September 20, 1958), the Poll tried to find out how this outlook copy was getting across to farmers who took one, two or three farm papers.

If a farmer took three farm papers, would this competition make him less interested in "What's Ahead?"

To find out, the Poll checked farmers who had Read Most of the copy in "What's Ahead."

Farm papers	No. of interviews	No. of readers	Per cent
Take *Wallaces Farmer* only	12	4	33.3%
Take two farm papers . .	46	16	34.8
Take three farm papers .	136	77	56.6

The big and important group was made up of those who took three farm papers. In this group, we found a higher percentage of readers of the department than in the other two groups.

A Purina ad for hog feed in *Wallaces Farmer* (September 20, 1958) raised the usual question: Did the ad get read by hog farmers who were good prospects? Any This Ad scores were used.

No. of hogs sold	No. of interviews	No. of readers	Per cent
None	27	5	18.5%
Less than 50	24	6	25.0
50–99	49	12	24.5
100 or more	92	33	35.9

Here the biggest group and the most important to the advertiser also made the highest score.

In some advertisements, the age of the prospect, whether he is an owner or renter, or whether he is in the upper third of income returns may be the important factor.

In a Purina hog feed ad in *Wallaces Farmer* (November 21, 1959) market analysis showed the following:

1. Younger farmers (21–34) were better readers than older ones.
2. Farmers with gross incomes of $10,000 or more were better readers than farmers with smaller incomes.
3. Farmers with fewer than 50 hogs sold during the year were the poorest readers.

In a Starcross Alfalfa ad in *Wallaces Farmer* (January 17, 1959) several breakdowns were used. The critical one probably was "Are you planning to sow alfalfa in 1959?" Any This Ad scores follow:

	No. of interviews	No. of ad readers	Per cent
Plan to sow alfalfa . . .	132	49	37.1%
Do not plan to sow alfalfa	65	16	24.6

Apparently the ad reached its target in a fair number of cases. But suppose the scores had been reversed and there had been 16 ad readers among those who planned to sow alfalfa and 49 among those who did not so plan?

The over-all score of 33 per cent would have been exactly the same, but the effectiveness of the ad would have been quite different.

A John Deere ad in *Wallaces Farmer* (January 17, 1959) checked corn acreage, income, total crop acreage and number of tractors owned (Figure 8.7). On the basis of corn acreage, the Poll found:

Any This Ad	No. of interviews	No. of ad readers	Per cent
No corn	21	8	38.1%
1–49 acres	55	23	41.8
50–74 acres	50	19	38.0
75 acres and up	62	39	62.9

The appeal of the ad was broad, but the bigger corn growers showed the most interest.

Another ad, Protein Blenders, *Wallaces Farmer* (January 17, 1959) was aimed at both hog and cattle feeders but did better with hog feeders than with cattlemen. With hog feeders the ad scored almost twice as high with those who sold 100 hogs or more as with those who sold less than 50. But with cattle, the feeders and the folks who didn't plan to feed came out almost the same (Figure 8.5).

The market analysis may throw additional light on split runs. A Bovitrin (Merck) ad on treatment for mastitis, *Wisconsin Agriculturist* (October 3, 1959), found the A ad scoring 20 per cent Any This Ad and the B ad, 32 per cent. Different illustrations were used — a test tube in A and a cow in B (Figures 4.4, 4.5).

These were men's scores for whole samples. But what kind of folks were the real prospects? Probably those who were having trouble with mastitis. A question on this found that 87 (55.4 per cent) of the sample were having trouble and the balance were not — or, at least, didn't admit it.

How did the ad appeal to those two groups? Scores follow for men:

	Had trouble		No trouble	
	A	B	A	B
Any This Ad . .	16.7%	47.0%	20.0%	20.0%
Read Some . . .	11.1	41.2	8.9	12.0

This indicated that the superiority of B over A was considerably greater in terms of prospects than was shown by the total score.

Market analysis of food ads brought out some useful facts. In *Wisconsin Agriculturist* (April 4, 1959) a check of the King Midas flour ad showed that families of four or more made up 59.5 per cent of the whole sample. But this part of the sample actually provided four-fifths of the persons in the households reached by the ad. A household with four eaters was worth twice as much as a household with two eaters. So the score of the flour ad with women in families of four or more was the vital item in the analysis (Figure 8.3). This group scored as follows:

	No.	Four or more in family Per cent
Any This Ad	70	58.8%
Read Some (Sales Copy) . . .	39	32.8
Read Some (recipe)	58	48.7

The Poll asked, "Have you done any baking in the last three days?" And 89.4 per cent of the sample said "Yes." These bakers paid more attention to the ad than the non-bakers.

This point was checked again with a Robin Hood ad in *Wisconsin Agriculturist* (April 5, 1958) (Figure 8.6).

	Baking — Yes	Baking — No
Any This Ad	**54.7**%	37.9%
Read Most (Sales Copy) . .	**18.0**	6.9

Another use of the market analysis shows up in a Ford Tractor ad in *Wallaces Farmer* (January 16, 1960). Here, among other things, the Poll asked the brand of the last tractor bought and then checked this reply against readership.

Any This Ad	No. of interviews	No. of ad readers	Per cent
Allis Chalmers	15	5	33.3%
Ford	27	13	48.1
International	62	14	22.6
John Deere	51	15	29.4
Massey Ferguson	8	4	50.0
Other	32	9	28.1

Of the 27 who had bought a Ford at last purchase, 13 looked at the ad. Of the 168 who had NOT bought a Ford at last purchase, 47 looked at the ad.

Ordinarily you expect that a user of a product will be more attracted to the ad than a non-user. The ad has two jobs at least: to renew the faith of the old customer and to attract a new customer. This Ford ad did well on both counts.

The critical point in using market analysis in advertising is this: What kind of breakdown will really throw light on the effectiveness of the ad? With feed ads, one question is obvious. Does the farmer who reads the ad have any hogs, or cattle or poultry or any other kind of livestock aimed at by the advertiser?

In some new products, age may be a factor. Young men will respond better than older ones. In some cases, income is important. A costly product won't stand much chance with a farmer of low income.

There is a temptation sometimes to use this kind of Poll as just another census. Since the number of questions that can be asked is limited (respondents run out of patience), the only questions used should be those that throw light on the specific ad being measured.

To get full value out of market analysis of advertisements demands study and cooperation between the advertiser and our research department. Properly handled, it can be one of the most useful of research tools.

Do young people read articles — and advertisements — as eagerly as older people? This is a vital question. The young farmers will be around for a good while. The older ones are getting close to retirement.

Suppose we had two articles, A and B. Each scored 45 per cent Read Most, which is good. But A had a 60 per cent Read Most score with young farmers and a 30 per cent score with farmers age 50 and over. Then suppose B had a 30 per cent score with young farmers and a 60 per cent score with farmers of 50 and over.

Which article would an editor prefer? Often the one which scored high with young farmers. (1)

Actually, most articles score fairly well with all age groups. This may be the result of editorial concern over the problem. Some reminiscent articles, like Bill

Groves' department in the *Wisconsin Agriculturist* or an article on bang-boards in *Wallaces Farmer,* are bound to score higher with older folks than with younger. But these are balanced by other articles and departments.

One of our surprises on age breakdowns is the high score made by younger people on social security articles. Apparently younger farmers valued the insurance features for widows and young children. They also seemed to think that social security for older farmers might lead to retirement and help younger men to farms.

Young men, in a weaker financial position than older, have been responding lately (1960) to articles that seemed to give hope for some improvement in income. A Washington report in *Wisconsin Agriculturist* (September, 1960), which told of plans for new farm programs, scored well for younger readers.

Wallaces Farmer checked on the effect of age on readership in the issue of February 4, 1961. Here are Read Most figures:

	21–34 yrs.	35–49 yrs.	50 and up
Men (20 items) . .	35.1%	39.1%	36.4%
Women (13 items)	36.2	41.4	41.1

This shows a fair score for people 21–34, but nothing to brag about. Editors would be happier if young people scored higher than older groups.

What about education? On this point too, the farm papers have been fairly successful in attracting both those with a grade school education and those who stayed in school longer. There are some differences. For instance in *Wallaces Farmer* (November 19, 1960) a somewhat technical livestock article showed a slight but not significant margin for farmers with more education.

A surprise came in a tax article in *Wisconsin Agri-culturist* (September 3, 1960) where the men who attended grade school only did significantly better than the other group. This may be a tribute to unusually clear exposition of a difficult but vital subject.

In the issue of *Wallaces Farmer* for February 4, 1961, articles and departments for men and women produced a mean Read Most as follows:

	1–8 years	9 years and up
Men (20 items)	30.6%	41.4%
Women (13 items) . . .	32.0	38.3

This seems to indicate that one of our problems is getting hold of the subscriber who has not gone beyond eighth grade.

How many of these folks are there? Of our Iowa subscribers less than half of the men and only about one-fifth of the women have stopped at eighth grade. In Wisconsin, around half of the men and two-fifths of the women are in this class.

This group shrinks every year. But for several years, at least, it is an important bloc. Are we shooting over the heads of those whose education stopped in the grades? What can be done to pull them in?

Do part-time farmers read different copy than full-time farmers? In one case in *Wisconsin Agriculturist* (September 3, 1960) an article on part-time farming did what you might expect. It drew a heavy vote from part-time farmers (64 per cent Read Most for men). Outlook copy (Agri-Vision) drew only 32 per cent Read Most for this group. On other items, part-time response was much like full-time.

These are points to remember:

1. The total score on an ad or article may not mean much. If a hog feed ad is read mostly by farmers without hogs, what good is it?

2. Market analysis can show whether the ad or article reached the folks at whom the copy was aimed.

3. Split runs may yield more meaning if we can find out how many real prospects read A and how many real prospects read B.

4. Watch the readership of young farm people. They are the subscribers of the future.

5. Subscribers who had only eight grades or less in school are not usually as good readers as those with more education. This is an editorial point that should be kept in mind in copy preparation and copy editing.

Figure 8.1

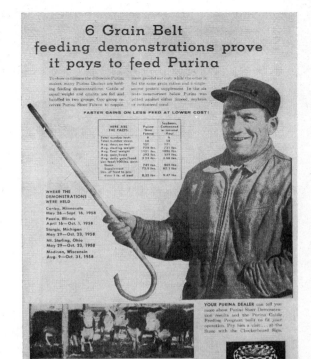

Page Score

Men 35%

Women 17%

Did Cattle Feeders Read?

This page advertisement had a fair score for all readers. The important point, however, is: How many farmers who were feeding or who expected to feed cattle looked at the ad?

Of the men readers of the issue, 39.3 per cent were feeding or planning to feed, 55.6 per cent were not feeding or planning to feed.

These two groups scored as follows:

	Any This Ad	Read Some
Feeding cattle	39.0%	18.2%
Not feeding	28.4	11.0

The cattle feeders showed more interest than the non-feeders.

Wallaces Farmer, January 17, 1959

Figure 8.2

Split A

Ad Score

Women 64%

The Balloon Went Down

In this three-column ad, the B picture with the balloon (to show a quotation) didn't do well. Here are the scores for women on the two pictures:

	A	B
Picture	55%	39%

The superiority of A on the illustration carried over into the copy. On the recipe at left, the Read Some scores were:

	A	B
Read Some	51%	41%

Figure 8.3

Split B

Ad Score

Women 49%

This test does not, of course, prove that the balloon is worse or better than the ordinary head. It does seem to show, however, that a good picture is weakened by cutting down space or introducing extraneous material. Don't mutilate a good cut!

The advertisement, taken as a whole, made a strong appeal to women with four or more in the family. These are the big bread eaters. The ad also did well with women who said they had baked in the last three days.

Wisconsin Agriculturist, April 4, 1959

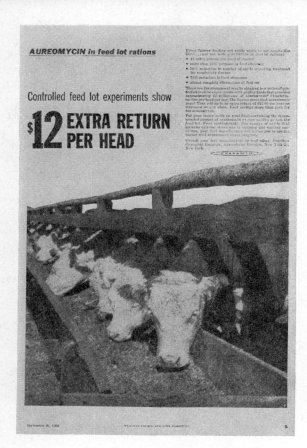

Figure 8.4

Page Score

Men 47.5%
Women 17.5%

Copy at the Top of Page

In several ads (some of them splits) we found that Sales Copy at the top of the page seemed to score better than Sales Copy lower in the page. What does this page ad show?

Score of the Sales Copy is good, but not outstanding:

Read Some 16.5%
Read Most 11.5

Question: Is the type too small to get full advantage from this position?

Cattle feeders paid more attention to the ad than non-feeders. Feeders gave an "Any This Ad" score of 63.4 per cent; non-feeders a score of 36.2 per cent.

Wallaces Farmer, September 20, 1958

Figure 8.5

Page Score

Men 37%

Women 8%

Big Hog Raisers Read the Ad

This page advertisement was aimed mainly at hog raisers, with a side shot at cattle feeders. The long sales copy (mainly a report of show winners) pulled a Read Some of 20 per cent. Attention was divided among five pictures. None scored very high.

The copy did hit the big hog raisers. Read Some scores follow for hog raisers who sold differing numbers of hogs during the year.

Less than 50 hogs sold . . .	13.2%
50–99 hogs sold	7.4
100 hogs or more	24.0

Cattle feeders and non-feeders did about the same amount of reading.

Wallaces Farmer, January 17, 1959

Figure 8.6

Ad Score

Women 60%

Cookies Score High

This ad (only 230 lines) scored as well as some much larger ads. Here are the Read Some scores for women on the Sales Copy and the recipe copy.

Sales Copy 43.0%

Recipe copy 57.5

The ad pulled well with all sizes of families. The critical point here, of course, is that a food ad must do well with the big families, those with four or more.

Age groups scored about the same. Younger women (21–34 years) seemed slightly less interested than older ones.

Pies and cakes rank a little higher with farm women than do cookies. But still over 40 per cent of Wisconsin farm women bake 4 dozen cookies or more in a week.

Wisconsin Agriculturist, October 3, 1959

Figure 8.7

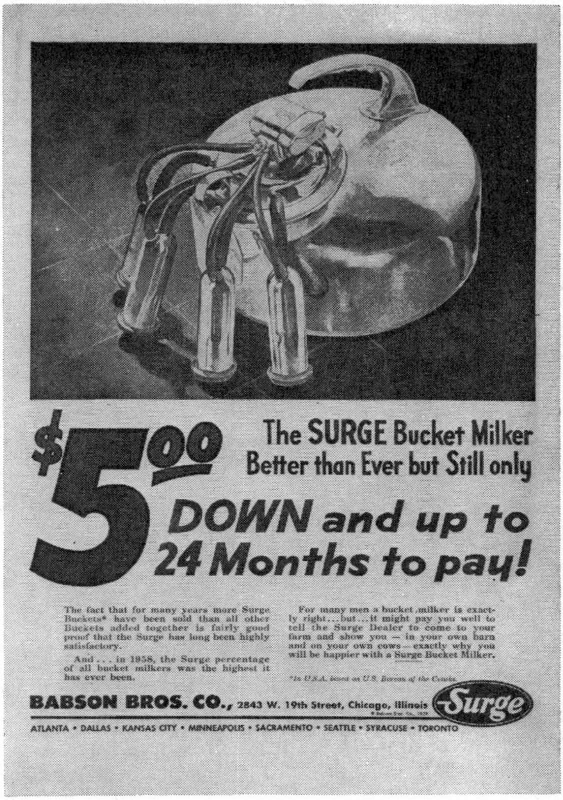

Page Score

Men 39%

Women 26%

Big Dairymen Read the Ad

Men gave the following scores to different parts of the ad, but the main interest lies in the response of the better prospects, the men with the big herds.

	Men
Any This Ad	39.0%
Picture	38.5
Head	18.5
Sales Copy Read Some	9.0

Of the farmers who were milking 30 cows or more, 56 per cent looked at the ad. The low score, 7.7 per cent, came appropriately from farmers who had no dairy cows. Farmers with gross incomes of $10,000 or more showed more interest in the ad than farmers with smaller incomes.

Wisconsin Agriculturist, April 4, 1959

Figure 8.8

Page Score

Men 46%

Women 14.5%

Bigger Farmers Read This Ad

What kind of farmers are the best prospects for an ad like this? Perhaps corn acreage may be a clue:

Men	Any This Ad
1–49 acres of corn . . .	41.8%
50 to 74 acres	38.0
75 acres or more	62.9

The bigger corn raisers paid the most attention to the ad as did the farmers with the biggest gross income and the farmers with the biggest acreage in all crops.

Sales Copy, with all farmers, scored 19 per cent. The illustration drew 43 per cent.

Wallaces Farmer, January 17, 1959

9.

The Problem of the Non-Reader

A NON-READER, IN OUR LANGUAGE, IS SOMEBODY who was exposed to the publication but didn't read it. He may, of course, be a reader for one issue and a non-reader for the next.

One man may have read every issue but the one that arrived at the peak of corn-picking time. If that issue is the one we survey, then he is a non-reader. Thus, the non-reader sample contains folks who never read the paper, some who read it once in a while and some who are good readers but just happened to miss this once.

Unsatisfactory as this is, the non-reader sample, accumulated over many surveys, still may give us some clues as to what kind of folks are hard to attract. Some clues are also given about the people who read the paper once in a while but not regularly.

In both Wisconsin and Iowa, non-reader figures have been assembled for several years. Older men and women showed a slightly greater tendency to be readers as contrasted with younger folks. More time to read may be more important than failing eye sight.

Years in school did make a difference. Scores (*Wallaces Farmer*) follow for 1958–60:

Education, men	Readers		Non-readers	
	No.	Per cent	No.	Per cent
1–8 grades . . .	358	38.5%	130	53.1%
9 grades up . . .	571	61.5	115	46.9
	929	100.0	245	100.0
Education, women	No.	Per cent	No.	Per cent
1–8 grades . . .	193	21.3%	96	28.8%
9 grades up . . .	713	78.7	237	71.2
	906	100.0	333	100.0

Non-readers were more likely to be found among men and women with from one to eight years of schooling.

In Wisconsin there is a similar picture. With women, the differences in schooling are not significant. Men, however, with from one to eight years of schooling are more apt to be non-readers.

These results can be looked at in two ways. If we are thinking about the subscriber of 1970, we want to be sure we are reaching farm people with high school education or better. These are the kind of folks we'll have in the future. But now and for some time to come, we'll continue to have readers who have only been to grade school. Can we reach them with simpler language, more pictures, etc. and still not lose readers with more education?

Mail boxes are flooded with newspapers, farm publications and general magazines. Is a non-reader one who is overwhelmed by a full mail box?

In Wisconsin, men taking three or more farm publications are more apt to fall in the reader than the non-reader class. The difference is significant.

Farm papers, men	Readers		Non-readers	
	No.	Per cent	No.	Per cent
Wisconsin Agriculturist				
only	92	11.7%	45	22.4%
2 farm papers	183	23.4	61	30.3
3 or more	508	64.9	95	47.3
	783	100.0	201	100.0

Women showed little difference, though the slight edge was in the same direction as with men.

In Iowa there was little difference with men, but women with three or more farm publications were more apt to be readers than non-readers.

Farm papers are not the only class of publications to compete for attention. The average farm family sees two or more general magazines. Does a farmer who sees *Reader's Digest,* or *Look* or *Time* stop reading a state farm paper? Does a farm wife who sees *McCalls, Better Homes and Gardens* or *Ladies Home Journal* stop reading *Wallaces Farmer* or *Wisconsin Agriculturist?*

We can't match the readers of General Magazine A against readers of *Wallaces Farmer.* The sample of readers of General Magazine A is too small. But we can sort out farm people who take one general magazine; those who take two and those who take three or more.

In Iowa we find that both men and women who see three or more general magazines are more apt to be readers than non-readers of *Wallaces Farmer.* Here is the women's score:

Women	Readers		Non-readers	
	No.	Per cent	No.	Per cent
1 general magazine . . .	177	19.9%	47	20.4%
2 general magazines . . .	188	21.1	71	30.7
3 or more	526	59.0	113	48.9
	891	100.0	231	100.0

In Wisconsin, men showed a slight but not significant margin in the same direction. Wisconsin women are apparently more likely to read general magazines. Those who took three or more general magazines are as apt to be non-readers as readers.

Three surveys in Wisconsin checked the effect of a second language on readers and non-readers. In general, a second language seemed to make no difference.

Men, second language	Readers No.	Readers Per cent	Non-readers No.	Non-readers Per cent
Germanic	127	58.0%	26	65.0%
Scandinavian	48	21.9	5	12.5
Other	44	20.1	9	22.5
	219	100.0	40	100.0

It should be noted here that of the whole sample about one-third had a second language. The table above has a small sub-sample for non-readers and any conclusion drawn therefore must be tentative. Women showed no difference between language groups.

Wisconsin Agriculturist ran another test on readers and non-readers. We asked each farmer to check the farm enterprise (hogs, dairy, poultry, etc.) from which he got 10 per cent or more of his income. On dairy products, beef and poultry, there was no difference. Farm men and women, however, who had 10 per cent of their income from hogs seemed to have more non-readers than one would expect.

Hogs, Men	Reader No.	Reader Per cent	Non-reader No.	Non-reader Per cent
	142	25.7%	34	38.6%

This is a small sample and should be observed with caution. Yet it seems possible that hog raisers may feel they are under-represented in the *Wisconsin Agriculturist*.

What do all these figures (details in editorial research files) show?

Both papers seem to be doing fairly well in a competitive situation with farmers who take many farm papers and many general magazines.

Wisconsin Agriculturist does a little better than *Wallaces Farmer* in keeping folks with from one to eight years of schooling. Yet the main need may be for both papers to be sure they hang on to farm people with a high school education or better.

On age groups, the important struggle is to hold those from 21 to 34 years of age. This is being done fairly well, but needs constant checking.

Figure 9.1

Copy Score

Read Some

Men 77.5%

Women 46.5%

Converting Non-Readers

Farm people who have been to school for only eight years or less are more likely to become non-readers than those who have gone to school longer.

Copy with strong appeal, especially to those who finished from one to eight grades, may attract some of these non-readers.

"What's Ahead" a department on market outlook in *Wisconsin Agriculturist,* had the following scores for men by education:

	1–8 grades	9 and up
Read Most	64.2%	72.5%

The average Read Most score for two-column articles in this issue was 32.1 per cent. So the 64.2 per cent score for those who finished one to eight grades is well above the average for this group.

Wisconsin Agriculturist, September 3, 1960

What's Ahead

Fall milk prices up

Milk prices should continue their way upward. But it's a seasonal increase. The climb will be less than last year's pace. The record flow per cow and a slow down in culling keeps milk production slightly above last year.

The number of dairy plants in Wisconsin continues to go down. There are now 1,302 plants in the state, compared to 1,776 in 1955; 2,528 in 1945. And the end of the decline is not in sight.

Net income per farm in Wisconsin stood at $2,561 in 1949. It worked its way up to $3,534 in '51 and then gradually slid back to a low of $2,147 in '55. Since that time it has gradually worked its way back up to $2,978 last year. It should again pass the $3,000 mark this year.

Ralph Yohe

It looks as if broiler prices will work their way downward through September. After that what happens depends upon the number of chicks going out.

If you have old corn to sell, you might as well sell it now. It looks now as if there's a big corn crop coming up. Prices at harvest time will probably run about 3 to 4 cents below last year's average.

Contracting for feeder cattle is way down this year. There'll be plenty of cattle available to buyers this fall. And buyers should be in a stronger bargaining position.

We'll see some weakness of potato prices in September. That's when the digging of the late crop gets underway. Get the late summer spuds out of the ground and on the market before the fall crop harvest starts.

The first phase of the beef cattle cycle—that of building up numbers—seems to be drawing to a close. Already the number of cattle going to market is increasing.

For the first half of 1960, cow slaughter was up 7 percent over last year, calf kill up 4 percent. Steer and heifer slaughter has been running about 10 to 12 percent ahead of 1959.

The average price of choice steers at Chicago last year was about $28. It'll be around $25.75 to $26 this year. Guesses are that it will go around $24—give or take a dollar—next year.

Outlook is still good for hogs over 225 pounds. But do everything you can to encourage fast gains over the next few weeks on hogs nearing market weight.

WISCONSIN AGRICULTURIST. September 3, 1960 (Volume 87, Number 17). Published semi-monthly by Wisconsin Farmer Company, Inc., Racine, Wisconsin. Subscription price, one year for One Dollar. Second class postage paid at Racine, Wis.

September 3, 1960

[148]

Take good care of baby pigs and you'll likely have larger, more even pigs at weaning time. Pigs above are on the Marion Steddom farm, Polk county, Iowa.

Baby pig care —it PAYS

"THE BETTER care you give your baby pigs, the better the pigs you'll have at 7-8 weeks of age," says Virgil Hays, Iowa State University swine nutritionist.

"Good baby pig management lowers death losses, and gives faster, more efficient gains."

Here are some points to follow for getting pigs off to a good start.

(1) **Shoot** for litters containing healthy pigs weighing 1½ pounds or more at birth. You can do this by keeping your sows in good condition, using a recommended ration.

"The main thing is to keep the sows in condition so they'll farrow and suckle large litters," says Marion Steddom, Polk county, Iowa, master swine producer. "And see that they don't get too fat."

(2) **Clean** your sows off and bring them into the farrowing house a couple of days before farrowing. This lets them settle down and get accustomed to the surroundings.

(3) **Start** sows on a good lactation ration containing about 16 percent protein after they farrow. Some folks limit feed to sows right after farrowing. Others let sows eat all the feed they want. It seems to work either way.

(4) **See** that pigs get a chance to nurse as soon as they are born. Tests show that pigs can take advantage of the antibodies in colostral milk for only 6 to 9 hours after birth.

(5) **Do** your ear-notching shortly after farrowing. It hurts pigs less then. And it gives you a chance to check each pig.

(6) **If** you've had trouble with navel infection in pigs, tie navel cords and clip them off, leaving the cord one-half to one inch long. Then dip them in iodine to stop infection.

(7) **Give** pigs a shot of iron dextran or iron dextrin solution at 3 to 5 days of age if pigs don't

have access to soil. This supplies them with iron until they get to eating dry feed.

"We give pigs iron whether we move them to pasture or not," explains Willard Lundahl, Boone county, Iowa. "We've tried pigs with and without iron—those getting iron do the best."

If you use pills or paste to supply iron, start treatment at 3 to 5 days of age. Then, repeat according to directions.

(8) **Let** pigs have early access to a good pig starter and see that they get plenty of fresh water to drink.

Here are Iowa State recommendations for pig starters.

For pigs to be weaned at 3 weeks, it's suggested you start as soon as possible on an 18 to 20 percent pig starter. Feed the starter until the pigs weigh 25 pounds before switching to a grower ration.

For pigs to be weaned at about 5 weeks, it's suggested you start them on a 16 to 18 percent pig starter at 10 days to 2 weeks of age. Then, feed the starter thru weaning until the pigs weigh about 30 pounds.

"Don't switch feed at weaning time," says Hays. "It just causes unnecessary stress.

"It's best to keep pigs on the starter for a week or so after weaning, then switch to the growing ration."

(9) **Don't** combine castration with vaccination or you may have trouble.

You may castrate pigs any time after they are a week old. The younger the better. It sets them back less.

Vaccinate for cholera and erysipelas any time after the pigs are about 5 weeks old. But avoid vaccinating within 10 days of weaning. Healthy pigs develop the best immunity.

(10) **If** you have pigs that fall behind while they're on the sow, you may want to take them aside and put them on a good pig starter.

February 4, 1961

Figure 9.2

Copy Score

Read Some

Men 60.5%

Women 20.0%

Hogs May Pull in Non-Readers

In Iowa, copy on hogs usually scores high. This baby pig article, for instance, had a Read Most score of 52 per cent for men. The average Read Most score for 20 articles and departments in the issue was 36 per cent for men.

Since those with from one to eight years of schooling are more apt to become non-readers than folks with more education, it is worth noting that men with one to eight years of schooling scored 45.2 per cent Read Most on this article. Copy with this appeal may help to make a regular reader of the subscriber who is inclined to look at the paper only now and then.

Wallaces Farmer, February 4, 1961

10.

Opinion Polls and Readership

OPINION POLLS, conducted by *Wallaces Farmer* and *Wisconsin Agriculturist* since 1938, have one obvious value for a farm paper. They provide timely articles with a local angle — "This is what Iowa farmers think about issue X; this is what Wisconsin farmers think about issue Y."

The polls can do much more than this. They give the editors insight into farm attitudes. They replace guesses on farm opinion with facts.

For instance, most of the editors on *Wallaces Farmer* assumed that Iowa farmers were "dry" in the sense of being opposed to state legislation for "liquor by the drink." Actually two polls showed a slight edge for such legislation; a third poll, a slight edge against.

Many students of political science recommend that the governor, like the president, be permitted to name his cabinet instead of having them elected. The same students recommend a four-year term for state officers.

What do farmers think? To date, farm opposition to these measures is strong, as measured by the polls.

This does not mean that the editors should drop the subjects. But it does mean that editorial discussion designed to favor these projects will have to do more than say, "This reform is a good thing."

The most important editorial use of the polls may be to measure areas of ignorance and indifference. We often use a screening question which asks, "Have you ever heard about Issue X?" Then we ask of those who have, "Do you approve or disapprove Issue X?" (1)

The original purpose of the screening question was to get rid of those who obviously had no right to an opinion. As it has turned out, the screening question does something more important. It indicates the area of ignorance.

In every poll, there is an "undecided" group. We used to be impatient with this response and tried to cut it down. Now we are inclined to think it has great value.

For example, in February 1960, the *Wallaces Farmer* Poll asked: "In the election this fall, Iowans will have a chance to vote on holding a constitutional convention in 1961. Have you heard or read anything about this proposal?"

Only 31 per cent said "Yes." The same question in August got a "Yes" vote of 27 per cent.

Plainly this was an area of ignorance. The polls indicated that there was a gap to be filled. Actually, while *Wallaces Farmer* did discuss the question, the effective work was done by the Iowa Farm Bureau Federation which conducted a vigorous campaign against the convention and carried farm districts in the election.

Contract farming began to get into the news in a

big way in 1958. It has already gone far in the broiler districts of the South, but hadn't affected the Corn Belt. In 1958, however, the *Wallaces Farmer* Poll described contract (integrated) farming as follows: "This is where a farmer signs with some company or cooperative to get help on feed, equipment, marketing, etc. and agrees in return to produce and sell much as the company or cooperative directs."

In July, 1958, men answered as follows:

1. 43% had heard or read a great deal about it.
2. 30% had heard some talk about it.
3. 37% hadn't heard it discussed.

This gave some support to the policy of using several articles in this field. While the issue wasn't as red-hot as we had supposed, a sizable majority had some information on the subject (Figure 10.1)

A larger area of indifference showed up in an August, 1959 poll on respirators: "Some farmers are using respirators to keep dust, chaff, etc. out of their lungs on especially dirty jobs. Did you make use of a respirator during the past year?"

Only 11 per cent said "Yes." Plainly, if the use of respirators is a good thing for farm health, it would take a lot of educational work to increase their use.

Another question in the field of health in *Wallaces Farmer* (February, 1958) was: "Have you been vaccinated for tetanus (lockjaw)?"

Over half — 54.5 per cent — said, "No." But even this result looked better than it actually was. Of the less than half who said, "Yes," most were vaccinated in the armed services and half of the "Yes" group were vaccinated 10 or more years ago. Apparently only about one-fourth or less of the total were effectively protected.

We run articles on fertilizer and get fairly good reader-interest scores. But how many farmers are prospects for such copy? In October 1958, we found that 37 per cent hadn't bought any commercial fertilizer that year. So an article on fertilizer, which assumed the use of fertilizer, was talking to only 63 per cent of our farmers. In 1958 some copy was still needed for farmers who hadn't bought fertilizer and who could only be reached by a different type of article.

In 1960 in Wisconsin milk quotas were being discussed. One of the issues was whether quotas could be transferred or had to stay with the farm. This was a fairly new and somewhat complicated issue. The poll asked:

"There has been some discussion of whether to make milk quotas transferable so that a farmer could sell his quotas to somebody else who wanted to keep a larger herd. Have you heard or read anything about this plan?"

Only 28 per cent said, "Yes, have heard something about it." The rest, 72 per cent said, "No, haven't heard."

Plainly the important news here (reported in *Wisconsin Agriculturist* February 4, 1961) was not how the informed farmers voted (almost half said quotas should stay with the farm) but that the majority hadn't heard about the proposal.

If transferable quotas were to be one of the farm policy issues, more discussion in the paper and elsewhere was needed before farmers could vote intelligently.

In 1958 in Wisconsin, there was much talk about dairymen changing over to the use of bulk tanks. Sometimes it seemed that everybody was changing over. To check, in October, 1958, the Poll asked: "How do you handle the milk pick up on your farm?"

Only 19.5 per cent said they used bulk tanks; 66.2 per cent still used milk cans. The rest (14.3 per cent) said they had no dairy cows.

Checkups of this kind show changes over time. On this bulk tank issue, a Starch survey in *Wisconsin Agriculturist* (November 5, 1960) found that 40.9 per cent had bulk tanks then. This can be contrasted with 7 per cent in September, 1955.

Somewhat the same question arose concerning the number of farms with milking parlors. Only 3.8 per cent of the sample reported using them in 1958. Apparently the popularity of this device had been overestimated at that time.

Integrated farming was also the theme of a Wisconsin question. In August, 1958, the poll reported 21 per cent had heard or read a good deal about it; 42 per cent had heard some talk about it; 37 per cent hadn't heard it discussed.

Apparently Wisconsin farmers were less interested in the subject than those in Iowa.

Trends were shown in political affairs. In July, 1953, 72 per cent of the Wisconsin sample said that Ezra Taft Benson was doing a good or fair job as Secretary of Agriculture. In August, 1958, 23 per cent voted this way. Iowa farmers showed a similar shift in the same years.

Questions on knowledge of foreign affairs were asked from time to time. Quemoy and Matsu were the subject of queries in both states before the 1960 presidential campaign. In 1958, 26 per cent of Iowa farmers "had been following the news closely"; Wisconsin had 33 per cent in this class.

Lebanon was a sore spot overseas in late 1958. *Wisconsin Agriculturist* asked: "Have you paid any attention to what's been going on in Lebanon, Jordan, and the Middle East?"

"Yes, keeping up closely" pulled 35 per cent; and 18 per cent said, "Haven't had time to keep up with it at all." The rest (47 per cent) were in the class: "Have followed it somewhat but have been too busy to keep up closely."

These examples show what editors can learn from the polls about the state of information of their readers. The surveys usually underline the old saying, "Never overestimate the information of your reader; never underestimate his intelligence."

The pre-test of subject matter also has a place in the editor's kit of tools. This is a device which uses a mail questionnaire to try to find out in advance how readers will respond to a given type of article.

This permits an editor to try off-beat subjects on a sample. Perhaps he has been timid about subjects in which people are really interested. At little expense, he can give such subjects a dry run and then — if the response is good — check further by an actual article printed in a survey issue.

We use a sample of 1,000 names. Returns run around 50 per cent. A white ballot "For the man of the house"; a pink ballot (same questions) "For the woman of the house."

Plainly, the 50 per cent who didn't answer were less

interested than the 50 per cent who did reply. We expected and usually got, higher scores on the pre-test than we could expect on a reader-interest survey.

As a rule of thumb, we said that the pre-test usually ran 20 per cent higher than the survey article. To be specific, when 80 per cent checked, "I'm sure I'd read this article," we expected a Read Most of 60 per cent.

This was a rough estimate and didn't always work out. Yet the pre-test did give some indication of probable results, and was helpful.

Sometimes it looked as if changes in the head (from pre-test to reader-interest) made a substantial difference. Here was a 1960 pre-test question:

"Hazards of going steady. Are young people who start dating early and settle down to going steady in high school more apt to get into trouble and find themselves pushed into marriage at 17 or less? Here are some case histories."

This had a pre-test score of 41 for men and 56 for women.

This subject was approached again, in the same pre-test as follows:

"Should we have 'shot-gun' marriages? When an unmarried girl becomes pregnant, often the family insists on getting her married in a hurry. But sometimes this merely loads the girl up with two or three more children and a bad marriage. What family experts say."

This, in essence like the first, pulled 44 for men and 76 for women. No change with men but a much higher score for women. The hotter head of the two pre-tests apparently made a difference.

An article in January, 1960, with the head, "High School Marriages" pulled 56 Read Some for men and

74 per cent for women. Read Most scores were 50 and 68. In this case, the pre-test came close to an accurate prediction of the readership score.

Since we have found that choice of subject matter is more important than any other factor, it seems that the pre-test might well be used more often. It gives insights as to reader response that can open up new fields to the editor.

Layout, style, illustrations and all the rest of the editor's tools mean little compared to picking the right subject. The reader-interest survey helps on this. So does the opinion poll. One rough test in the opinion poll is to see how many comments were volunteered by respondents on a given subject. If a question brings out 30 or 40 comments, as reported by interviewers, the chances are that the subject has more reader appeal than one that only brings out a dozen comments.

But the pre-test still does the best job in helping the editor check on the interests of his subscribers that he might otherwise ignore. Often he will find that a subject to which he hadn't given much thought will rank high.

What the pre-test can't show is what will interest farmers five or 10 years from now. This is the subject of Chapter 13.

The opinion poll and the pre-test, of course, should not be used to scare editors away from subjects in which only a few farmers are interested. The paper should always be a few jumps ahead of its readers — but not too many.

In 1918, *Wallaces Farmer* ran a good deal of copy on hybrid corn. Probably only a few farmers were interested. But the hybrid corn copy — continued until hybrid corn was on the market — undoubtedly played a part in preparing for the boom in hybrid corn in the thirties.

Again, in 1922, *Wallaces Farmer* began to pound hard on the theme that overproduction was hurting farm income. Suggestions were made on ways to adjust production to demand. Again the editor was considerably ahead of farm opinion and of farm organization leaders. But the early discussion of the issue made for more general acceptance of the AAA later.

One great editorial danger is that the editor, up to his ears in a subject, may think everybody has the same interest and the same background he has. This is rarely true and this assumption may lead to articles and editorials that leave out data important to the understanding of the issue by the average subscriber.

The opinion poll helps to keep the editor conscious of this hazard.

Advertisers run into the same problem. An ad may play up a theme that a farmer has heard too often. It may play up a theme of which he has never heard. Both kinds of ads may lose.

*   *   *

Here are some points to keep in mind:

1. An opinion poll tells the editor what farmers think about current issues.

2. It also tells him which issues they haven't heard about or in which they aren't interested.

3. The pre-test of subject matter helps the editor on his most important job, the selection of subjects that interest his subscribers.

Figure 10.1

Page Score

Men 72%

Women 46%

The figure shows a Wallaces Farmer page titled "Farmers vote NO on plans for contract (integrated) farming" with an article "What farmers say about contract farming."

Photo, Box, Article

Did readers look at the box, ignore the photograph and the article and turn to the next page? Or did they look at the photograph only and ignore the box and the article?

Men	No.	Per cent
Saw picture only	8	4.0
Saw picture and article	102	51.0
Saw box only	2	1.0
Saw box and article	104	52.0

At this time, 27 per cent of the men hadn't heard about contract (integrated) farming. So the article started with the handicap of trying to attract some readers who were unfamiliar with the subject.

Wallaces Farmer, September 20, 1958

Figure 10.2

Men 80.2%

Women 42.0%

Poll Articles Rank High

This is the report of a *Wisconsin Agriculturist* Poll on a proposed change in dairy policy. The article was given a high score by men and a fair score by women. Both wanted to know what other farmers thought about production quotas.

	Men	Women
Read Most	59.9%	19.1%

The article appealed to men of all ages:

Read Most	21–34 years	35–49 years	50 up
	63.6%	54.5%	63.0%

Education seemed to make no difference in the response. Farmers who had quit school at eighth grade and those who had gone to high school and beyond scored about the same.

Wisconsin Agriculturist, April 5, 1958

11.

Subjects That Appeal

WE HAVE NOTED that selecting subject matter is the major task of the editor. If the reader is excited about a subject, he'll endure bad writing, small type and unattractive layout.

To discover the most attractive subject matter, the editor can pre-test themes, as suggested in Chapter 10.

He can also, within limits, rely on past experience with readership tests. It is always necessary to remember that a subject exciting in 1960 may not be exciting in 1961, and that a subject full of attraction in November may be old and dull the following April.

One of the most complete studies on subject matter was conducted by the Statistical Laboratory of Iowa State University in three editions of "InFARMation Please" (1947, 1951 and 1955). (1) In each of these surveys around 600 farmers and 600 farm women were used in a probability sample of Iowa farm operators and homemakers.

The study was designed to find out where farm people go to get information. It also showed the kind of farming and homemaking information in which farm people were interested.

In the first study (1947) farm operators were given a card listing 11 subjects. Each was asked to "read off the five things for which you most often need and use information."

The subjects and the number of farm operators choosing each are shown in the summary below:

Subject	Farm operators choosing subject	
	No.	Per cent
Handling and feeding livestock . . .	387	69.48%
Market prospects a year or more in the future	334	59.96
Advice on present livestock and grain markets	303	54.40
Corn and other field crops	252	45.24
Care and use of farm machinery . . .	239	42.91
Contouring, terracing, drainage, etc. .	201	36.09
Repairing and constructing barns . .	176	31.60
Farm accident prevention	155	27.83
Keeping poultry	126	22.62
Corn loans and other federal farm programs	82	14.72

Field work was done in the fall of 1947. This was a year farm prices and income were good. Probably for that reason the interest in "corn loans and other federal farm programs" was low. The editor, thinking of the high interest in such programs in the 'thirties, was inclined to overestimate farm interest in the subjects in 1947.

Market outlook ranked high and resulted in some changes in copy and in editorial emphasis. Although *Wallaces Farmer* had always given special weight to these subjects, it seemed possible that we should do even more in that field.

At the same time, farm women were asked similar questions:

	Farm homemakers choosing subject	
	No.	Per cent
Recipes and meal planning	370	69.42%
Canning and preserving food	361	67.73
Patterns, sewing and fashions	322	60.41
Home improvement	294	55.16
Keeping poultry	275	51.59
Health and medicine	247	46.34
Kitchen and home equipment	232	43.58
Gardening	225	42.21
Child care	172	32.27
Beauty care	52	9.76

There were few surprises here. It looked as if the usual concentration on food in *Wallaces Farmer* was justified. We did wonder why the low score on "beauty care." Did farm women think it unwomanly to admit an interest?

The next survey of this kind was in November, 1951. Had times changed? Did farmers and farm women have different interests?

Four choices were given to each farmer. Note the top four in the men's list:

	Farm operators choosing subject	
	No.	Per cent
Marked prospects in months ahead . .	316	53.5%
Fertilizers and rotations	312	52.8
Handling and feeding livestock . . .	286	48.4
Weed and insect control	258	43.7

Fertilizer was coming to the front. The chemical revolution in weed and pest control was on the way. Corn this time was down to 9th in a list of 12.

Women had changed less. The top four were the same. But "health and medicine" had come up a notch. A vote was not taken on "beauty care."

In November, 1955, another survey was made. The top subjects for men were as follows:

	Farm operators choosing subject	
	No.	Per cent
Market prospects in the months ahead .	360	54.9%
Current livestock and grain markets . .	296	45.1
Handling and feeding livestock	294	44.8
Price supports, farm legislation, social security, etc.	275	41.9

"Fertilizers and rotations" was in fifth place and "weed-insect pest control" in seventh. Observe the steady appeal of market information and the rise of "price supports, farm legislation, etc."

Farm income in 1955 in Iowa was still good, but it was starting down from the peak. Hogs in Iowa, in November, 1955, were down to $11.60. This was quite a change from the May price of $17.00 and the peak price in April 1954 of $26.40.

Women's choices stayed about the same with one striking exception. "Health and medicine" came up to third place. There were 326 women, or 52.4 per cent of the total who selected this subject.

It looked as if *Wallaces Farmer* was justified in running more copy on price supports and more on health and medicine than in 1947 or 1951.

A readership survey supported this view. In October 1, 1955, the readership survey checked a page article entitled "Ask $17 Support for Hogs." The page as a whole pulled 87.5 per cent with men. The article had a 64.9 Read Most score for men. It also drew a fair number of women readers, 28.5 per cent Read Most. Women, on this and other occasions, indicated that they knew where the money for their new washer was coming from — or if it was not coming.

Readership scores in survey issues underline the same points. In *Wallaces Farmer* (February 4, 1961) a page of discussion of market trends and of management problems pulled 84.5 per cent of the men, with a Read Most of 66.5.

A three-column article on page 72, "Insurance for Hospital Bills" got Read Most scores of 28.5 per cent with men and 44.0 per cent with women. This article was outside the Home Department, aimed at women, but also drew some men.

The importance of timely news was shown in *Wallaces Farmer* (November 19, 1960) when a two-column Washington Letter, headed "What Will Farmers Get From Kennedy" pulled 64 per cent Read Most for men and 33 per cent for women. A post-election analysis of the farm vote in the same issue got 56 per cent Read Most for men and 39.5 for women. (Incidentally, this proves again that farm women do a lot of reading outside the Home Department.)

The same issue illustrates treatment of a subject of interest only to a minority. A two-column turkey article got a Read Most for men of 15.0 per cent and 14.5 for women. This was a deliberate play to a small group.

Another example of outlook copy registering high came in *Wisconsin Agriculturist* (April 15, 1961). The two-column department "What's Ahead" got a Read Most of 68.5 for men and 30.0 for women.

A page article appealing to smaller farmers, in the same issue, was, "He Farms 60 Acres." This had a page score for men of 72.5 and for women of 62.5, with a Read Most of 59 per cent and 43 per cent. This article was a mixture of farm management and human interest. Its main appeal probably was to farmers who were uncertain about the ability of a man farming 60 acres to make a living.

Another *Wisconsin Agriculturist* (April 2, 1960) shows the usual response by farm women to a food article. The page score was 92 per cent for women and Read Most 71 per cent. A few men, as usual, gave a quick glance at the illustration (pancakes) and went on hastily. We can get women to read men's articles but have a hard time getting men to read women's articles. The exception is when the Home Department lead deals with family problems and is illustrated by photographs in which men appear.

Dairymen are a minority in Iowa, just as hog farmers are a minority in Wisconsin. So when *Wallaces Farmer* (January 16, 1960) devotes a page to dairy farming, a high score is not expected. In this case the market was further narrowed by the title, "Stanchions and Pipeline Milking" which didn't apply to all dairymen. But the page score still was 43.5 per cent for men and 34.5 for women. Read Most was 22.5 for men and 14 for women.

Outlook copy scored high on both papers. An example is "What's Ahead" in *Wallaces Farmer* (January 16, 1960) where the two-column department pulled 76 per cent of the men and earned a Read Most of 66 per cent. Some women, 28 per cent, were also interested.

Figure 11.1

Page Score

Men 87.5%

Women 47.5%

When Hog Prices Hurt

A timely subject will bring the readers in. In 1955, there was a sharp drop in hog prices. The *Wallaces Farmer* Poll asked farmers about federal action on hog supports.

The resulting article was read by both men and women:

	Read Most
Men	64.9%
Women	28.5

The top pictures scored 78.6 per cent with men and 42 per cent with women. The bottom picture scored 54.8 with men and 26.5 with women.

Wallaces Farmer, October 1, 1955

Figure 11.2

Page Score

Men 20.5%

Women 77.0%

Better Light in the Home

Food copy always scores high with women, but so do articles built around home improvement. Here is an article about lighting the farm home. Women responded well; a number of men also read it.

Read Most score for women was 60.5 per cent. Also important was the fact that women of different ages responded about the same way.

	Women 21–34 years	35–49 years	50 years up
Read Most . . .	50.0%	48.6%	52.8%

Women who had gone to school for eight years or less scored as high as women who had gone to high school or beyond.

Wallaces Farmer, February 4, 1961

What does our experience with subject matter add up to?

1. Hit hard on the major interests of your audience. This means hogs and corn in Iowa and dairy cattle in Wisconsin. But try for new material and new angles. A dairyman doesn't want to read about cows every issue unless the material is timely, fresh and loaded with human interest.

2. Keep checking on the interests of readers. You know that when hog prices drop sharply, interest in hog outlook and hog supports will pick up. But other angles are harder to figure out. Why, for instance, did women's interest in "health and medicine" pick up? For information on some points, you have to dig, use opinion polls and pre-tests of subject matter.

3. Don't forget minorities. In a hog state, you can't give as much space to sheep as to hogs, but sheep still are entitled to some attention.

4. Farm people are human. Articles on family problems score well. And even a dirt copy article gains when the problems are stated in terms of Henry Brown of Black Hawk County and Jim Jones of Keokuk County.

12.

Just Getting Read Isn't Enough

WHEN *Wallaces Farmer* BEGAN its first readership studies in 1938, we could say that a certain number of readers of the issue had actually read some or most or none of the article on page six or the advertisement on page 21. But presently it dawned on us, as on many others, that this kind of readership figure wasn't enough.

Fortunately, the readership survey can be handled so as to tell us much more. We can find out how readership is affected by age, education and other factors. We can even approach a more vital question: What do our subscribers think of what they read?

A reader may go through an article and still wind up with a poor opinion of the article and of the magazine. High readership may be associated with either favorable or unfavorable response. How can we find out which it is?

We are using on *Wallaces Farmer* and *Wisconsin Agriculturist* some simple devices that may give us some clues as to what farm readers think of what they read.

We started out with the most obvious of tests. In repeated surveys, conducted both by ourselves and by the Statistical Laboratory of Iowa State, we have found that farmers want practical information on timely production problems. The perfect tribute to us comes from the farmer who says, "I was just going to write you. But when I got your paper out of the mailbox, I found you had answered the question I had in mind."

So in the reader-interest survey of the January 18, 1958 issue of *Wallaces Farmer,* we prepared a card that asked these questions:

If you read most of the story, "Wet Corn Makes Top Feed," on page nine how would you rate this article on the points below?

1. Real practical help for me.
2. A few things here I can use.
3. Nothing practical here for me.

1. Article told about something new to me.
2. I'd heard about it before, but not as much.
3. Nothing new in this article.

In this test, we hoped to find out whether the article was of practical help, and also whether some of the information was new. These points, in our minds, weren't the same. A farmer could be reminded of standard information and still get practical help.

Interviewers waited until they got to page nine and listened to the report of the respondent on that page. If he said he had read most of the wet corn article, he was handed the card.

Here is the response:

	No.	Per cent
Real practical help for me . .	32	24.1
A few things in it I can use . .	70	60.1
Nothing practical here for me	21	15.8
	123	100.0
Article told about something new to me	29	23.6
I'd heard about it before, but not as much	80	65.0
Nothing new in this article . .	7	5.7
No comment	7	5.7
	123	100.0

Since this was the first attempt, we weren't sure what it meant. What is par for the course? Our guess was that the article did pretty well.

To check again, we took the reader-interest survey of *Wisconsin Agriculturist* (April, 1958) . When the interviewer got to page 76 and the respondent indicated he had read most of the article, "Spray Yellow Rocket in Hay Fields," he was given a card which asked him to rate the article. Scores for men follow:

	No.	Per cent
Real practical help for me . .	20	23.0
A few things in it I can use . .	40	46.0
Nothing practical here for me	18	20.7
No comment	9	10.3
	87	100.0
Article told about something new to me	25	28.7
I'd heard about it before, but not so much	41	47.1
Nothing new in this article . .	5	5.8
No comment	16	18.4
	87	100.0

To get a little more light on what to expect from a "practical help" vote on a dirt copy theme, we asked the same questions about three articles in *Wallaces Farmer* (January 17, 1959). The three scored an average vote on "real practical help" of around 38 per cent among the men who read some or most of the copy. If we measure these enthusiastic readers against the whole sample, they made up 25 per cent of the total.

What kind of men were these enthusiastic readers? There were 77 men out of the sample of 200 who voted "real practical help" on one or more of the three articles. These enthusiastic readers had slightly more education, more income, took more farm papers and had bigger farms than the non-enthusiasts.

We had another problem allied to this one. On it, we used a similar device. We were running two departments about whose merits we were doubtful. For the test, we added a third department whose long-time record was excellent and on which we had no doubts at all.

To the folks — both men and women — who read some or most of the three departments, the interviewers handed out a card which said:

The editors of *Wallaces Farmer* are wondering whether to drop this department. They'd like your advice. Which of the statements below comes nearest to representing your views:

1. Don't take the department out. I like it very much.

2. I usually read it, but I could get along without it.

3. Take it out if you want to. I won't care.

4. No opinion.

We had interviewer trouble on this one. Some interviewers didn't present the card to all the Read Somes and Read Mosts. But the main disappointment was the general amiability of the comments. Very few wanted to get rid of any of the departments. The following scores list those who said, "Don't take it out."

	Men		Women	
	No.	Per cent	No.	Per cent
Workday Pointers	103	86.5	63	80.1

(**This was the strong department, according to other tests.**)

Rural Route Ramblings . .	93	77.5	82	78.8

(**This was the department, humorous in intent, on which we had doubts.**)

Country Air	32	80.0	82	85.4

On this test, all three departments earned the right to stay in. However, I'm not satisfied with the answer. Maybe our respondents were too amiable. A less brutal third choice than "Take it out" might have showed us more about farm attitudes.

We had another problem with the department dealing with recipes. Readership scores don't show much about recipe reading. Scores are always high. But surely there are differences between one set of recipes and another. Yet you wouldn't think so from the usual scores.

In the reader-interest survey of *Wallaces Farmer* (January 17, 1959) (Figure 12.6), we had interviewers find women who said they had read some or most of the recipe column. Then each respondent who had read the department was given a card which said:

Since you read some or most of this Cookery Corner department,
I'd like to know a little more about your use of the recipes:

1. Have you tried out any of the recipes on this page?

                    1. Yes   2. No

2. If Yes, how did the family like the recipe?
        1. Liked it   2. Didn't like it   3. No comment

3. Are you planning to use in the future any of the recipes on
   this page?

            1. Yes   2. No   3. Undecided

A similar study was made in *Wisconsin Agriculturist* (April 4, 1959). Here are the results for both papers:

	Wallaces Farmer		Wisconsin Ag	
	No.	Per cent	No.	Per cent
1. Have you tried out any of the recipes on this page?				
Yes	34	24.3	41	26.6
No	106	75.7	113	73.4
	140	100.0	154	100.0
2. If Yes, how did the family like the recipe?				
Liked it	26	65.0	32	55.2
Didn't like it . . .	2	5.0	7	12.0
No comment . . .	12	30.0	19	32.8
	40	100.0	58	100.0
3. Are you planning to use in the future any of the recipes on this page?				
Yes	82	62.1	133	82.1
No	19	14.4	6	3.7
Undecided	31	23.5	23	14.2
	132	100.0	162	100.0

The main value of the experiment was to establish a base line that would mean more than the standard one: "Every recipe column should get a Read Most score from 60 to 65 per cent." Now we are inclined to say, "If less than 20 per cent of the recipe readers have tried out a recipe in the column, we're slipping."

Another study of women's readership came in *Wallaces Farmer* (January 16, 1960). We ran an article about selecting, cooking and serving a prime rib roast (Figure 12.5).

The Poll asked: "Have you ever cooked and served a beef roast in the way described?

	No.	Per cent
Yes	51	41.5
No	72	58.5
	123	100.0

We found here that our farm women were less familiar with this kind of meat cookery than we had guessed.

We also asked: "If No, did the article make you want to try it some time?"

	No.	Per cent
Yes	68	80.7
No	9	10.9
Undecided	7	8.4
	84	100.0

Apparently a large number were interested in trying out what, for them, was a new method in cooking meat.

The Poll also asked: "Would you like to see more articles of this type in *Wallaces Farmer?*"

	No.	Per cent
Yes	121	95.3
No	2	1.6
Undecided	4	3.1
	127	100.0

The editors learned that there was a demand for this kind of copy and that for many women, it was a fairly new field. We had not expected as many to be unfamiliar with the subject; neither had we expected so much interest in more articles.

The over-all score (Read Most 56.5 per cent) was good, but it did not convey any of the information secured through the questions above.

Advertisers are even more anxious than editors to find out whether farmers believe what they read. In a reader interest survey of *Wisconsin Agriculturist* in 1959 one advertiser asked us to find out whether farmers believed the claims in copy about the efficiency of the feed being advertised.

We found 47 men in the sample who had read some or most of the ad copy, and who expressed an opinion on the ad. These men were given a card which restated the claim in the ad. We then asked the respondent to check one of the following:

1. Sounds reasonable to me.
2. Might be possible, but I'm not sure.
3. Don't think you could do it.
4. Undecided.

Of the 47 men who checked an answer to the question, 19 had serious doubts about the claim. The scores follow:

	No.	Per cent
1. Sounds reasonable to me	7	14.9
2. Might be possible, but I'm not sure . .	17	36.2
3. Don't think you could do it	19	40.4
4. Undecided	4	8.5
	47	100.0

This seemed to show that the claim in the ad wasn't getting across. A change in copy was indicated.

Another advertiser wanted to find out whether a testimonial, using the picture and name of a farmer, was believed. This MoorMan's ad appeared in the *Wallaces Farmer* (September 20, 1958) (Figure 12.2). The card asked whether an average farmer could be as successful in feeding hogs as was the man in the testimonial. There were 42 men who read some or most of this copy. They expressed themselves as follows:

	No.	Per cent
1. Yes, seems likely	22	52.4
2. No, he was lucky	10	23.8
3. I didn't pay much attention to his experiences	10	23.8
	42	100.0

While the sample is smaller than we like, the testimonial does seem to get a fair vote of confidence. Of the 42 farmers who read this copy, 20 were large hog raisers who had marketed 100 hogs or more in the past year. Of these 20 prospective buyers of hog feed, 14 accepted the testimonial and only two rejected it. This approval by men who were presumably the better prospective buyers of hog feed gave additional weight to the results.

Another advertisement also ran testimonial copy on a feed ad. Farmers who read the ad were asked, "You've read the report of the experience of John Doe in feeding livestock. Do you think it likely that he could really do this well?"

The farmer readers of the ad answered:

"Yes, I think he could probably do that well" . . .   43%
"Seems like the ad claims a little too much"   . . .   35
"It claims a lot too much"   8
"No opinion"   14

This advertisement had a good readership score. But was the believability score high enough? The advertiser had some doubts. The copy is getting another look.

In the three feed ads discussed above, much the same kind of sales argument was used.

In all three ads, layouts were of almost equal merit. All three had good readership scores. What made the difference in believability?

One of the lower ranking ads ordered the farmer to buy the product and shouted in large type what the benefits would be. The better ad tackled the theme with this head:

"Good results — as reported by Marvin Gesell, Howard County, Iowa."

The copy following gave a detailed report of what happened on the Gesell farm. The conclusion —

reached in the twentieth short line under the head —
presented a feed cost about the same as that reported
in one of the less successful ads.

Questions can throw more light on reader response
to articles. Two articles may have the same readership
score. Yet one may be enthusiastically received and the
other cast aside with the bored remark, "That's old
stuff."

Tests like these have the great merit of being fairly
easy to handle in connection with a standard reader-
interest survey. They answer, easily and inexpensively,
one of the major questions every editor asks about
readership. (1)

Figure 12.1

Page Score

Men 72.5%

Women 44.0%

"Help" and "Enjoyment"

Men who read this department were asked, "What did you think of it?"

"The article made suggestions that
will be of practical help to me" 42.3%
"It has a few points I can use" 32.4

Men readers were also asked whether they enjoyed reading the article — thus, "enjoyment" as contrasted with "help." And 92.8 per cent of readers of the department reported they "enjoyed" the copy.

Farmers may find it harder to admit "help" than "enjoyment." Both sets of questions throw some light on the meaning of the readership score.

Wisconsin Agriculturist, April 15, 1961

Figure 12.2

Page Split A

Page Score

Men 42%

Women 26%

"Did You Believe Gesell?"

These two pages came out almost even in scores, with one marked exception. The sales copy in B, pushed up to the top of the page, did better with men (Read Some 27 per cent to 16 per cent) than the sales copy in A.

Readers of the page were also asked, "Do you think an average farmer could be as successful in feeding hogs as Mr. Gesell was in the case reported here?"

Over half (52.3 per cent) answered, "Yes, seems likely." Other experiments on the believability of testimonials indicate that a 50 per cent approval is an unusually strong vote of confidence.

Figure 12.3

Page Split B

Page Score

Men 48%

Women 24%

Women showed less interest in the ad, more skepticism about the testimonial. Only one-third of the women readers of the ad said, "Yes, seems likely."

The A reader may note that this cutout did about as well as the square photograph. This is contrary to the result in Figures 4.10, 4.11. In that case, the square photograph out pulled the cutout. One explanation may be that in 12.3, no damage was done to the hogs; in 4.11 the cows were badly chopped up. The mutilated cut in 4.11 destroyed the appeal of one part of the photograph; in 12.3, the hogs were allowed to make their usual appeal.

Wallaces Farmer, September 20, 1958

Figure 12.4

Copy Score

Read Some

Men 65.5%

Women 33.5%

High Production is the rule in this herd owned by John and Kathryn Bartlett, Winnebago county. Good milking and feeding practices have helped to bring record production.

Good Management Means More Milk

*Feeding and milking practices h
big influence on dairy product*

FEEDING and milking practices influence more milk records than any other management factor.

That's the report from University of Wisconsin dairy specialists who point out that the difference between poor and excellent milking practices alone is around 100 pounds of butterfat per cow every year. That amounts to 3,000 pounds for a 30-cow herd.

"Production records are now being broken because of better feeds and better management," points out E. E. Heizer, University of Wisconsin dairy specialist. "In past decades, high energy feeds weren't considered as important and cows just weren't producing at the highest rate possible."

**Regularity Is Important
to Good Management**

Some dairymen like Oliver Propst, Dodge county, consider regularity one of the most important management points.

"Chores come first on my farm," he says. Once you get a system, sudden changes are hard on the cows, so I like to be as regular with milking as possible."

The Propst herd was one of 43 Wisconsin Holstein herds analyzed by researchers to pin down the degree to which milk and fat production are influenced by "environmental factors."

Specialists rated each of these herds on regularity, availability of feed, vacuum levels on the milking line, sanitation, udder stimulation, milking machine time and mastitis control. Results were combined with other feeding and management practices.

Taking care of dry cows was one of the important production-boosting practices investigated. Within reasonable limits, say the specialists, days in the dry period are not a total loss as far as production is concerned.

"I like to give my cows about 60 days dry period," says Nelson Mason, whose Dodge county herd was surveyed by investigators.

In the study, cows receiving eight weeks rest period averaged around 10 pounds more fat during the next milking year than those

which had dry periods of three weeks. For a 30-cow such as Mason's, this could around 300 pounds more fa year.

Of the factors studied, ade feeding and milking pra seemed to be the most impo If you underfeed cows by one pound of TDN daily, the researchers, you'll be around 12 pounds of fat pe per year on the average. 30-cow herd, that's about pounds of fat each year.

How you feed is even mor portant than how much you Cows in a herd where fe practices rated excellent produce some 75 pounds mo during the year than if they in a herd where the feeding tices rated poor. For a 30 herd, this could mean more 2,000 pounds of fat yearly.

The study also underscore advantage of large cows and with a long productive life herd. Seven cows in the Joh Kathryn Bartlett herd in W bago county proved that po January when their total lif production went over a m pounds of milk.

**Takes 40 Average Cow
to Equal 7 High Ones**

Dairy experts point out t would take 40 average U. S. to equal the million pound time mark of the seven Ba Holsteins.

It should be remembered cows don't reach their h level of production until the 6 or 7 years old. And they c decline to any extent for at five years.

This points up the val keeping cows in the herd as years as possible.

But for most dairymen, counts is the combined infl of inheritance and enviro (feeding and management tions).

The cow that's going to you the most money is one bred for high production, managed in such a way th can produce at the peak e inherited ability.

Wisconsin Agriculturist, October 3, 1959

"Will These

Methods Work?"

Men who read this article on dairying were asked if they thought "the methods reported would work on my farm."

Of the men readers of the article, 43.7 per cent said "Yes." And another 22.2 per cent checked, "These methods might work on my farm." Only 6.3 per cent said, "They wouldn't work on my farm."

Cookery Corner

Cottage Cheese Salad

1 package lime gelatin
2 cups cottage cheese
¼ teaspoon salt
Juice of ½ lemon
Small can crushed pineapple (drained)
½ cup chopped nuts
1 pimento sliced (canned)
Make gelatin according to

directions on package. Let set until firm and beat until fluffy. Add rest of ingredients. Put into salad molds (individual or large one) which have been rinsed in cold water. Let set. Serve on salad greens. Can be topped with a maraschino cherry.

Baked Stuffed Pork Chops

4 rib pork chops (cut 1 inch thick)
1 tablespoon chopped onion
¼ cup diced celery
2 tablespoons fat
2 cups dry bread crumbs
½ teaspoon salt
Dash of pepper
¼ teaspoon sage
½ cup water
Salt and pepper

Slit a pocket along the bone side of each chop. Prepare the stuffing by browning the onion and celery in fat and then combining with crumbs, salt, sage and water. Stuff each chop with this mixture. Season chops, place in a baking pan. Cover pan and bake in a 350 degree oven for one hour. Uncover and continue baking 30 minutes to brown.

Stuffed Cabbage

1 large head cabbage
1 lb. chopped beef or half beef and half sausage
1 egg
3 sliced onions
½ cup bread crumbs
¼ cup catsup
Salt and pepper to taste

Fry onions slowly in butter until soft and yellow. Add

chopped meat and stir with a fork for 5 minutes. Combine meat mixture with egg, catsup, bread crumbs and seasoning. Stuff cabbage that has been topped and cored. Replace the top and tie cabbage securely with clean string. Steam about an hour in a small amount of water or until cabbage is tender. Serve with sour cream.

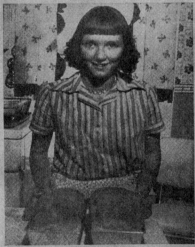

WANDA MILES, Ida county, Iowa, exhibits some of her home baked bread. Wanda says that, of her high school studies, home economics is her favorite.

January 17, 1959

WALLACES FARMER

Figure 12.5

Department

Score

Women 88.5%

They Tried Out Recipes

This department "Cookery Corner" always has a high score. But what does the score mean?

One way to find out is to ask, "Have you tried out any of the recipes on this page?" The women were interviewed from 10 days to two weeks after they received the paper. Of the women readers of the department, 24.3 per cent answered "Yes."

And 62 per cent said they planned to use one or more of the recipes in the future.

Wallaces Farmer, January 17, 1959

Figure 12.6

Page Score

Men 11.5%

Women 85.0%

"Do You Want To Try This?"

Women readers on this page were told about selecting and cooking a prime rib roast. Then they were asked, "Have you ever cooked and served a beef roast in the way described?"

Less than half (41.5 per cent) said, "Yes."

We also asked, "If No, did the article make you want to try it some time?" Of this group, 80.6 per cent said they'd like to try it. And of the whole number of readers of the article, 95.7 per cent said they'd like to see more articles like it in the paper.

Farm women were less familiar with this kind of cookery than we had guessed. They were also more eager than we had expected for more copy of this kind.

Wallaces Farmer, January 16, 1960

From this series of ads and from similar studies, is it possible to draw any conclusions that will help copy writers to anticipate trouble in this field? Plainly more data is needed, but the following suggestions may be helpful:

1. The best ad didn't claim too much and didn't shout too loud. An almost diffident approach, coupled with a conservative claim, seemed to help believability.

2. Testimonial copy apparently can be either good or bad. It is bad if it sounds like the farmer quoted was bragging. A farmer talking across the fence to his neighbor doesn't brag too openly. He is more apt to say, "I was lucky this year. Got a bigger crop than usual."

3. Easy reading of copy is important. In terms of a Flesch "reading ease" score, the copy lead in the top ranking ad had 13 words to the sentence and 132 syllables per 100 words. The copy lead in one of the other ads had an average sentence length of 20 words and a syllable count of 156 per 100 words.

4. If the advertiser's experiments show that he can, most of the time, cut feed costs 50 per cent under those shown by the average farm, this is good news for the product. Yet it may not pay to make so strong a claim — even if well documented — in the ad. Farmers discount big claims.

5. Copy that issues orders: "Buy this, etc.," is not likely to do as well as a more indirect approach that says, in effect, "John Doe is doing pretty good with this feed. Maybe you'll have the same experience."

13.

Research in the Future

THERE HAS BEEN A REVOLUTION in farming since 1940. Bigger farms, new machinery and new methods have made enormous changes. A good farmer of 1940 who left Iowa, went to California and came back to Iowa to farm again in 1960 would be baffled by many of the things he would have to do.

In this period of rapid change on the farms, have farm publications changed? Critics insist that the farm paper of 1940 is almost the same as the farm paper of 1960.

We use larger type, more and bigger pictures, and grow breathless in pursuing the latest developments from college experiment stations and from the experimenters of commercial concerns. Have we changed enough?

The evidence is that farm publications still hold farm interest. The series of "InFARMation Please" reports, prepared by the Statistical Laboratory of Iowa State University, indicate that farmers still rely heavily on the state farm paper as a source of information.

Other surveys show much the same thing. Glenn Johnson of Michigan State reports on sources of information by 1075 farmers in seven Midwest states. (1)

Information on Prices

	No. of mentions
Farm magazines	856
Publications of farm organizations	160
Newspapers	664
Radio	635
Television	145

Information on Production

Farm magazines	513
Publications of farm organizations	75
Newspapers	195
Radio	196
Television	57

Information on New Technology

Farm magazines	242
Publications of farm organizations	24
Newspapers	89
Radio	72
Television	29

In the opinion of these farmers, what are the "most important" subjects?

	No. of mentions
Prices	352
Production method	325
New technology	64
Human information	79
Institutional	92
Couldn't rank first	8

On production, the bread and butter of the content of farm publications, the high standing of the farm press seems clear. On prices — and price prospects — newspapers and radio are pushing up. On new technology, the farm press leads. Yet it should be noted that new technology ranks low in prestige compared to production and prices.

Why are farm papers, even if relatively unchanged since 1940, still doing so well in their traditional role? It might be noted here that every editor will probably say that his farm paper has changed since 1940; it is the other papers that have not changed. Most outsiders looking at the issues of the two dates would say, "Yes, some changes. But a reader of 1940 would still feel at home with the paper of 1960."

One reason for the continued strength of the farm press is probably just habit. Probably every farmer in Illinois grew up in a home where *Prairie Farmer* came regularly. To a degree, the same is true of the *Wisconsin Agriculturist* in Wisconsin and *Wallaces Farmer* in Iowa.

The stock remark of an older subscriber is often, "I did my first reading in your paper. Looked at the livestock pictures and puzzled out the words alongside."

Over the years, too, each farm paper has been able to do something useful for most subscribers. Another stock remark: "You had a piece in the paper 10 years ago that I tried out and it worked. I figured it paid my subscription for 20 years."

A Starch report in *Wallaces Farmer* (March 5, 1960) asked the question: "Have you ever made use of farming or homemaking ideas (including recipes) reported in *Wallaces Farmer?*" Of the men, 65 per cent said "Yes" about farming, and of the women, 68 per cent said "Yes" about homemaking.

The reverse is also true. A farmer who didn't buy an extra 80 in 1940 because of the paper's conservative warnings may calculate how much he lost by not gambling on a rise in prices during the war boom. A Republican farmer who voted for Hoover in 1932 might be critical of a paper's support of the New Deal's farm program.

On the whole, however, the farm publication is an old friend, or if not an old friend, at least an old and familiar enemy. There are always subscribers who open the paper eagerly to "see what this blankety-blank-blank is going to say this week." And even one of these subscribers may add, "This guy is crazy on politics, but he does know something about corn and hogs."

But is familiarity with the product always an asset? Perhaps there are young farmers who think the familiar paper is too old-fashioned and "says the same thing over." The young farmer is geared to television, to more general magazines, to more farm papers, to more time on the road and in town and less time in a chair by a reading light. This is an additional reason for a continued check on the reading habits of young farmers.

Add to this the fact that there are more kinds of folks in the country than there used to be. There are residential farmers, who live on 10 acres and have a horse and a few chickens. There are retired farmers. There are part-time farmers who keep some stock and do a little farming on week ends but whose main income comes from a job in town. In the ranks of commercial farmers, there is a great difference in interests between the man with a gross income of $5,000 a year and one with $40,000 a year.

Farmers were more alike in the old days than they are now. The 1960 census raises the question of the nature of the farm audience. Will editorial copy that registers with the 6.7 per cent of Iowa farm operators who are part-time farmers also register with the 4.6 per cent who take in $40,000 or more?

The census figures on economic class indicate how income groups line up in the two states:

	Iowa		Wisconsin	
	No.	Per cent	No.	Per cent
Class I (sales of $40,000 up)	8,110	4.6%	1,010	0.7%
Class II				
($20,000 to $39,999)	21,579	12.4	4,221	3.2
Class III				
($10,000 to $19,999)	48,045	27.5	23,750	18.1
Class IV ($5,000 to $9,999)	47,408	27.1	43,523	33.2
Class V ($2,500 to $4,999)	23,537	13.5	28,324	21.6
Class VI ($50 to $2,499)	5,655	3.2	5,868	4.5
Part-time operators, etc.	11,660	6.7	16,392	12.5
Retirement, etc.	8,701	5.0	8,114	6.2
	174,695	100.0	131,202	100.0

Do we want to put out a farm paper that appeals to all these folks? It is possible, but it has difficulties. The part-time farmer and the big commercial farmer are both interested in rural schools, in the social problems of country living, in flower gardens and lawns. But the description of an automatic feeding set-up wouldn't mean much — except as a curiosity — to farmers below the gross $10,000 level. To include farmers above that level would mean an audience of around 44.5 per cent of the Iowa total.

From the business angle, all of these people are a market for consumer goods — overalls, shoes, groceries, household gadgets, etc.

Would it make more sense to aim a farm paper at the better commercial farmers? If we aimed at the interests of those with $10,000 or more, this would be 44.5 per cent of the census total in Iowa and 22.1 per cent in Wisconsin. If we stretched it to include those with an income of $5,000 or more, this would be 71.6 per cent in Iowa and 55.3 per cent in Wisconsin.

There is another way to deal with this problem, of course. Shift to the vertical approach. Get out a farm paper devoted exclusively to dairying, or to hog raising or to poultry raising. Yet in the Middle West, most of the farmers have more than one major interest.

These are policy questions for the publishers and the editors. But the questions may get better answers if more research is carried out. Just how does our circulation now break up? How many are part-time farmers, how many are town people who own farms, etc?

What kind of copy are the bigger farmers reading? What kind is read by smaller farmers? So far our investigations show that production copy gets much the same kind of response from big and little farmers. But how many readers do we lose when we talk about a problem that affects only the top 10 per cent of our farmers? How many do we lose when we talk about a problem that means something only to the lower 10 per cent of our readers? We need to continue investigations in this field.

In checking on the appeal of vertical publications, we need to know the readership habits of farmers who sell 150 or more hogs a year and of farmers who milk

30 or more cows. We have a good deal of information in this field, but it should be kept up to date.

Editorial style is related to these other policy decisions. Will it be useful to follow the lead of *McCalls, Better Homes and Gardens,* etc. and run less copy in very big type? How reconcile the interest of the man who wants a detailed technical article with the interest of the man who prefers only a 200-word summary?

How important is the slick paper, four-color format to subscribers? (We know already that it is important to most ad agencies.) Our slick paper, four-color inserts give us a chance to compare the appeal of this kind of advertising copy with the appeal of run-of-the-book ads. We have no way at present to use splits to check editorial appeal of the two kinds of presentation. Experiments by others indicate that four-color layouts do not always help readership.

Another problem deals with the farm woman's interest in the paper. At present, we get fantastically high readership scores on Home Department copy and good scores for women on copy aimed primarily at men. Farming is, in many cases, a family affair. Women participate in decisions. With more education than men, they often point out to husbands articles they should read or ads they should notice.

Yet in the business field farm papers lose ground in advertising directed to farm women. Farm women use lipsticks, and only a fraction of the farm audience takes any one women's magazine, yet cosmetic advertising misses farm papers. Farm women buy groceries for hearty eaters in big families, yet food advertising is light.

Is the answer to forget about farm women and aim copy only at farm men? Or is it to continue to appeal to farm women and hope that we can get more information on the farm women's market to the agencies? This question is also related to the question of dealing with commercial farmers only or with everybody living in the country. All women living in the country have similar problems — in gardening, in canning and freezing and in relation to rural schools.

Every publisher and editor should probably devote special time to a consideration of the death of *Country Gentlemen, Cappers Farmer* and a score of other farm publications. What killed them? Is there any chance that we have the same disease?

That is one good reason for more editorial research and for more thinking about the results of editorial research.

More emphasis should undoubtedly be given to pre-testing new subject matter and themes the publication has never used. To rely exclusively on earlier readership surveys is to be chained to the past.

Farm publications may be tied more to the past than other magazines. For them, the argument is even stronger for using pre-tests of subject matter as described in Chapter 10.

Something might be said here about the claim that "you can't edit a paper with a slide rule." Some folks worry about editors being influenced by experiments like ours to the extent that individual initiative, intuition, and possibly genius, will be stifled. (2)

There is some risk here, but I doubt if it adds up to much. A very few editors may decide that the results of a readership experiment (not always statistically significant) should be followed blindly. Far more will disregard such experiments and be guided, as usual by their own hunches, by habit, by the examples set by their contemporaries and by a few letters from subscribers.

Both extremes are foolish, of course. Anyone who has read this book this far will note how tentative many of our conclusions are. Many experiments do no more than provide the editor with a hunch. But a hunch of this origin may have value.

I remember the comment made by one eminent statistician when I was worrying over tests of significance. He said, "Let's suppose this experiment doesn't have results that turn out to be statistically significant. Still it is all the evidence you have to go on. If the cost of making the change indicated by the experiment is small, better go ahead and make it. And then run some more tests."

Figure 13.1

Page Score

Men 54%

Women 28.5%

Who Were the Best Prospects?

This advertisement scored well. Its Read Some for men on sales copy was 27 per cent. Read Most was 19 per cent.

To which farm groups did the ad make the strongest appeal? Farmers who were young, with good incomes and on bigger farms showed the most interest.

Crop acres harvested	1–49 acres	50–74 acres	75 acres and up
Read Some	38.1%	46.9%	64.3%

Of the 98 farmers interviewed on this question, 63 had 75 acres or more. This was the biggest as well as the best market.

Wallaces Farmer, January 16, 1960

Figure 13.2

Page Score

Men 61.5%

Women 34.5%

Who Reads About Farm Records?

Younger farmers and farmers with larger incomes were more apt to read about farm record keeping than older and poorer farmers.

Read Some scores on men's age groups follow:

21–34 years	35–49 years	50 and up
75%	63%	45.3%

Here are Read Some scores on income groups:

Under $5,000	$5,000–$9,999	$10,000 and up
44.7%	69.6%	70.7%

Farmers who had gone beyond eighth grade in schooling were more interested than farmers whose education stopped earlier.

Wisconsin Agriculturist, April 15, 1961

The great danger in editing is not the blind following of experimental work. The great dangers may be these:

1. Doing this year exactly what you did last year and failing to test new ideas;

2. Imitating some drastic change made by a contemporary publication without testing its appeal to your particular audience;

3. Being influenced by a few letters, some from folks with an ax to grind and some by a few subscribers who are either radically for or radically against some proposal;

4. Failing to try to look five or ten years ahead, to try to see what audiences and publications may be like then;

5. Forgetting that sociology, anthropology, psychology and history are also fields in which farm editors need skills. Farm families are people as well as hog raisers and corn raisers.

*   *   *

Do readership surveys, pre-testing and opinion surveys help farm publication editors to avoid these dangers? I think they may. Every time a readership survey upsets a cherished belief, the editor is likely to profit.

"If I'm wrong about this," he may say to himself, "I may be wrong about something else." And he should be more able to take a fresh look at his job.

14.

What Kind of Editor?

ANY DISCUSSION OF READERSHIP tests should close by repeating the usual warning. A readership test measures the past. An editor may in June of 1963 get out exactly the kind of publication that scored high in 1962. But 1963 is not 1962. There will be resemblances, but there will also be differences. How do you figure these out?

Before trying to answer this question, let us look for a moment at what I have called the "Joe Ratner Formula." Ratner was a talented editor who worked with *Better Homes and Gardens* and later with an advertising agency. He believed in research. He used it. But he also could laugh about its limitations.

"This is the way it works," Joe said. "You believe in readership research. So you check on the last issue. Food copy ranked high. OK, you throw out everything but food copy. Now in the next issue, you find that pie recipes outscore everything else. So you fill the next issue with pie recipes. But your readership survey shows that apple pie recipes score higher than others. The result is that the next issue, the climax of readership testing, includes nothing but apple pie recipes."

This is ridiculous, but true. Every readership expert should repeat it to himself regularly.

What you need, of course, is balance in the issue. In a farm publication in Iowa, we are sure that corn and hog copy will score high. But that doesn't mean everybody wants to read only about corn and hogs. Minor interests play a part. So does variety.

But the major problem is still: What kind of new copy will attract your readers?

The pre-test of subject matter, already described in Chapter 10, is one way of estimating short-run changes. If the editor is bright enough, he can set up a number of possible subjects and have these checked by the reader.

But how does he know which subjects to ask about? Surveys on opinion and readership can give him some clues, but only clues. He needs to generate some ideas himself.

He can borrow ideas from other magazines. This is often a risky business since editors sometimes run together like sheep in what may be the wrong direction. The pre-test may help to show an editor that he is running the wrong way. This has value, even though it is negative value.

The editor can read widely, talk to people with different views, visit farmers and then think, "What can we say next issue that will do this fellow and his wife any good?" And he can use the pre-test to check his hunches.

So far we have been looking ahead in 1962 to what will be timely and useful in 1963. Now we come to a much harder task. How do we, in 1962, manage to look ahead to what will be timely and useful in 1965 or 1970?

My best example concerns Henry A. Wallace and his articles on hybrid corn. He began to write about hybrid corn in 1918. We had no readership tests then. If we had, my guess is that the score would have been low. Yet Wallace kept on writing on this subject which gradually became important. By 1934, when hybrid corn was first used, farmers knew much more about it and were quicker to use the new strains than if Wallace had waited 10 years to begin discussing the subject.

You can make the same point about economic issues. I'll use Wallace again as an example since he is the editor about whom I know the most. In 1922 he began to hammer on the need to adjust production to market demand. This program did not result in actual legislation until 1933.

Does it pay an editor, or his publication, to be five or ten years ahead of his times? Franklin D. Roosevelt, an expert in political affairs, used to say that a political leader should be a year or two ahead of the public, but no more.

An editor perhaps should follow the same rule. Yet I think there is an argument for letting readers know what is in the air, and what is likely to happen some years in the future. For this kind of copy, an audience will grow.

How can farm publications get the kind of editorial talent that can look ahead? If they get this kind of talent, can it be turned into circulation and into advertising lineage?

There are some doubts on this second point. I knew

one man active in the business end of a farm publication who said flatly that the job of the editor is to fill in the white spaces left in the dummy after the ads are placed. He insisted that he saw no relation between editorial copy and circulation or between editorial copy and advertising appeal. (Perhaps he did see this relationship, but felt it better business to ignore it while arguing over editorial salaries.)

Circulation is not solely a matter of editorial appeal. It depends, to a great extent, on the skill and persistence of the circulation department. Editorial appeal does make renewals come easier. A paper that isn't read with interest cannot be boomed by even the most skillful circulation campaign.

Advertising readership, of course, is dependent on the ability of the editor to get readers to go through the issue and give an advertiser a chance. I can recall one "expert" who insisted that he wanted an ad placed opposite a dull article, so that the article wouldn't distract attention from his ad.

One constant question is: Are we getting out a paper for the readers or for the advertisers and the advertising agencies. Very often a layout that appeals to an agency falls flat when exposed to readers. And editors may be led into editorial blind corners by an agency's art director who has never checked his layouts against farm readership.

Finding first class editors is a problem and holding them is more difficult than it used to be. Editors are often persuaded into going with ad agencies, public relations firms, house organs and the like. This has been a good break for the journalists. They can bargain for pay and fringe benefits. But this situation has often lost farm papers the kind of editorial talent they can hardly afford to lose.

Pay in money isn't the only temptation. An editor is paid by prestige, by the feeling of power and by the satisfaction in making policy and influencing readers. Men — and women — who don't get this kind of pay are apt to move.

There are different kinds of editors, of course. One is the amiable kind, who knows everybody, whose editorials irritate no one, and who has the skill to introduce new ideas into the reader's head without the irritations that usually accompany that process.

Then there is the editor who fills up space, who goes through the motions and whose paper reads like everybody else's.

The most useful editor may, according to my biased view, be the one who is able to look a few years ahead and to get his readers ready to accept the future or perhaps to modify it. He needs to know more than agriculture. He should know how United States agriculture fits into the affairs of the nation and of the world.

Here are two quotations that seem to me to indicate the kind of thinking that farm paper editors — and all editors — ought to be doing.

Lawrence E. Hinkle, Jr. said after describing the authoritarian way of life,

The point might well be made that the conflict between this way of ordering a human society and its opposite — the open system of thought, based upon observation, constantly tested against reality, allowing for great uncertainty, accepting a variety of points of view, not pretending to know the ultimate right or good and always keeping open the possibility that any judgment is incorrect — may be the basic conflict of our time. (1)

I think a farm paper editor ought to be on the side of the "open system of thought." He should be thinking also about Kenneth E. Boulding's "traps for the future." Boulding of University of Michigan said,

The three traps are war, population and exhaustion. A nuclear war if it did not put an end to man, might easily remove from him any chance of perpetual affluence. Unlimited growth of population could do the same thing more slowly but just as effectively. The ghost of Malthus has been laid many times, but it won't lie down.

If science and technology give us death control, it must also give us birth control. We must eventually have a stable population and if we are all going to live to be 70, the birth and death rate cannot be more than about 14 per thousand. This means an average of a little over two children per family and no nonsense.

The third trap might be our inability to develop a non-exhaustive high-level technology. Our existing technology is essentially suicidal so far as it is based upon geological capital which we are rapidly squandering. We cannot build permanent affluence on fossil fuels, not even uranium, and still less upon deposits of ores.

Permanent affluence must depend upon fusion as a source of energy, either in the sun or here on earth and it must depend upon the use of this energy to concentrate the diffuse elements of the sea and the atmosphere. Fortunately this high-level technology seems almost in sight. It is perfectly possible, however, that either nuclear or population explosions might prevent us from ever attaining it. (2)

I do not suggest that every editor should agree with Boulding's statement of the problems or of their treatment. I do suggest that these are the kinds of subjects on which a good editor should spend some time and thought.

It is not enough to know that 9-point type on an 11-point slug will get more readers than 9-point solid or that a picture six inches square will get more attention than a picture three inches square.

These — and their cousins and their brothers in research — are tools to be used by an editor who has something to report that may be useful to his readers, his nation and folks in other lands. While he must write with today in mind, it is hoped that he can also keep in mind the needs of 1970 and even the needs of the year 2000.

Survey Methods and Reports

15.

Survey Methods

SURVEY RESULTS are no better than the methods used. Many readers, therefore, will want a description of the methods used by *Wallaces Farmer* and *Wisconsin Agriculturist*.

I started in 1938 by getting advice from the Iowa State University staff. Ray Jessen, Arnold King and T. W. Schultz helped in laying out the program.

We began by taking the economic regions of the two states, as defined by the U. S. Department of Agriculture and by trying to give each region its proper representation in the sample. For instance, the dairy region of northeastern Iowa has 20.6 per cent of the farms. We aimed, therefore, to interview 20.6 per cent of the rural-farm adults in that region.

Within each economic region, we selected from six to eight counties to represent different soil types, ethnic groups, etc. Within each county, we told our interviewer (a farm woman) to work on one mail route (in reader-interest surveys) or on one road or in designated townships (in opinion surveys). The interviewer was instructed to begin interviewing outside town and suburban areas and to stop, without exception, at every other farm house along the route.

This sample, it will be noted, is not a strict probability sample. We did experiment with that kind of sample. The Statistical Laboratory at Iowa State drew up the design and we sent interviewers to the exact farms designated. Bad roads and call backs created problems, and finally we dropped back to the method described above.

We continually check our sample against census data and against U.S. Department of Agriculture crop and livestock reports. For the most part, they match. We have trouble from time to time with interviewers who pick the better farms. We alleviated this problem partially by emphasizing "every other farm" at training sessions. One complication comes up in bad weather. When a farm lane is filled with snow, the interviewer is likely to ignore the "every other farm" rule.

When we began the work, we asked interviewers to skip farms of 30 acres or less. In time, however, it seemed clear that this instruction had, at least, two errors. No interviewer can tell from the road how big the farm is. Our papers needed to know about small and residential farms as well as large ones. In recent years, therefore, the interviewer stops at all farms. We then sort for the small farmers, part-time farmers, full-time farmers, etc.

An example of the check against census data is the report made for the reader-interest survey of March 17, 1956 in Iowa.

The sample was made up of 200 men and 200

women on Iowa farms of 30 acres and over. The sample compares with census figures as follows:

Corn Acres	Survey	Census
30–49 acres	43.2%	40.3%
50 and up	56.8	59.7

In owners and renters, the sample compares with the census as follows:

Tenure	Survey	Census
Owners	65.5%	61.6%
Renters	34.5	38.4

In crop acres planned for harvest in 1956, the sample compares with the census as follows:

Crop Acres	Survey	Census
30–99 acres	32.3%	40.2%
100 and up	69.7	59.7

It should be noted that we continue to have trouble with farm size. It is possible, of course, that the sample has kept pace with the rapid shift toward larger farms and is more accurate than the outdated census figures we are forced to use. In 1961 our sample in Iowa had 72.4 per cent in the "100 crop acres and up" class while the 1959 census had 64.5 per cent.

Comparisons with "intention to plant" and "pig survey" estimates by U.S. Department of Agriculture have helped us to check our sample. More difficult is the regular check on farm voting. To get the farm vote in the state, we use the 1950 report on rural-farm adults in townships. We assume that townships in Iowa with 85 per cent rural-farm adults are representative of the farm vote; in Wisconsin, we use 80 per cent rural-farm townships.

Since the 1960 census did not make a report on rural-farm adults by townships, we adjusted the township figures by throwing out all townships which had population increases since 1950.

The problem in an election, of course, is not only to get a true sample of the rural-farm population but also to find how many and what kind of people are going to vote. This affects the size of the sample used. In order to be sure of interviewing around 500 voters, we must interview 700 people. In rural Iowa and Wisconsin, around 75 per cent of the eligible adults go to the polls.

After the election, we check back on the actual vote cast in the rural-farm townships. In 1960, for instance, we estimated that Nixon would get 56 per cent of the rural-farm vote in Iowa. He got 54.4 per cent. In Wisconsin, we estimated 50 per cent for Nixon. He got 52.4 per cent.

One result of the accurate pre-election polls is that we learn a good deal about the kind of people who vote for each candidate. How did young farm people vote? Catholics? Protestants? How many split their tickets?

We use, of course, two kinds of samples. One — for opinion surveys — deals with all farm people. The other — for reader-interest surveys — deals with subscribers only. Iowa and Wisconsin subscribers are so nearly representative of all farmers that there is little difference between a subscriber sample and a total farmer sample. A census investigation and breakdown some years ago in Iowa found our subscribers on slightly larger farms and with somewhat more livestock and income than Iowa farmers taken as a whole. (1)

Whether a survey is accurate depends to a great degree on the skill and the probity of the interviewer. From the beginning we have used farm women. They work for us only a few days a year, of course. We make two reader-interest surveys a year and from two to four opinion surveys. We select these interviewers on the basis of advice from farm friends and county extension people. We bring interviewers into Des Moines (in Iowa) and into Madison (in Wisconsin) for training sessions.

When a survey is completed, we send a letter of correction and approval with the check. There is some turnover. Some of the young women have babies. Some older ones find interviewing difficult in winter. A few are dropped because they cannot follow instructions. The kind of farm woman who is aggressive enough to enjoy knocking at strange doors must also listen and try not to convert the prospect. Some are incurable and leave us.

The farm woman interviewer has many advantages. She isn't turned down. By saying, "I'm Mrs. Smith; I live on a farm the other side of Blankville," she puts herself in a different class from the ordinary business caller. And she quickly adds, "I'm not selling anything." We forbid interviewers to accept any money for subscriptions.

In split runs we actually use two samples. Again, think of Iowa counties as a checkerboard. We send A copies to the black counties and B copies to the red counties. The interviewer must be warned to stick to a mail route originating in the county in which she is assigned.

We have changed methods since we started. At first we used a fresh copy of the paper for every interview. The interviewer marked with pencil the items noted. This method created problems in the office, for it was difficult to translate this kind of data onto IBM cards. We used homemade devices of various kinds, but finally shifted to a method outlined by Professor Robert Jones of the University of Minnesota in *Journalism Quarterly*. (2)

Every part of every article or ad had a code number, and these code numbers were repeated on a score card which was marked by the interviewer. Then IBM punch operators took these score cards and put the data on IBM cards. This made it possible to get detailed breakdowns on our sorting equipment.

What difference did the change in methods make in scores on copy? It is difficult to be certain, but my impression is that the present method pushes up the Any This Page scores a little. The code numbers point to different parts of the article or ad and force the respondent to ask himself, "Did I look at that?"

In a split run, we try to match one kind of copy in the A version against a different kind (preferably with only one factor changed) in the B version. We use for split runs a sample of 100 men in A and 100 women in A; an equal sample in B.

How can we tell if the difference between A and B scores means anything? Suppose, for example, that the A version has a Read Most score of 45 and the B version a Read Most score of 60. Is that difference significant?

In statistical tests of this type, the hypothesis under consideration is that there is no difference between the copy used in the A and B samples. Differences between the A and B groups may be obtained owing to chance fluctuations arising from several sources.

The practical question we ask is: Is the difference

between the A and B groups large enough so that it is unlikely to have arisen from chance fluctuations alone. We have used a 5 per cent level of significance as the cutting point for evaluating such a difference. Thus, if a difference is large enough so that it would be expected to occur only one time in 20 as the result of chance fluctuations, we are inclined to accept it as indicating a real difference in readership.

We also need to look at the scores on unchanged copy. Suppose the article tested is on marketing corn and is on page 14. Let's see how unchanged copy nearby with a similar theme compares.

	A	B
Page 10 — Editorial on corn	40%	45%
Page 12 — Farm letter on corn . . .	30	35
Page 16 — Ad on seed corn	15	20
Page 18 — Hog rations using corn . .	50	60
Total	135	160
Average	33.75	40.0

This difference in the scores of the controls should be taken into consideration in estimating the significance of the split itself.

Does the split run, in the example noted above, mean anything? Note the 15-point difference in favor of B in the split and the 6.25-point difference in favor of B in the controls.

The split-run difference here may still mean something, but we'd feel much better if we ran another split. If another split — and perhaps another — also shows a pattern with B ranking consistently ahead of A by 10 points or more, we are probably justified in accepting the result.

Another way, when possible, is to duplicate the experiment. On page 14, we print Change X in A; on page 54, we use a similar article and a similar change, but run Change X in the B version. This — other things being equal — should wipe out the differences between A and B on unchanged copy.

This duplication of splits is possible with editorial copy. It is difficult to arrange with advertising copy. Yet even with editorial copy, one can't be sure of exact duplication.

If heads are being tested, are we sure that the head on a dairying article will have exactly the same relationship to copy as the head on a hog article? Dairymen may read one; hog farmers may read the other. These are different groups, and they may react to heads in ways related to their occupation. A difference in head scores may only prove that dairymen and hog farmers have different tastes, not that one head is better than another with all readers.

It is still possible to make a series of splits on a particular point with all the conditions as nearly alike as possible except for the tested factor. If, time after time, we get about the same answer, we can be fairly sure that, for our audience, the experiments indicate what we should be doing. An example is our series on a second color. Another is the earlier series on Flesch scores.

One colleague suggested I repeat a paragraph from Chapter 13. I wrote:

"I remember well the comment made by one eminent statistician when I was worrying over tests of significance. He said, 'Let's suppose this experiment doesn't have results that turn out to be statistically significant. Still it is all the evidence you have to go on. If the cost of making the change indicated by the experiment is small, better go ahead and make it. And then run some more tests.' "

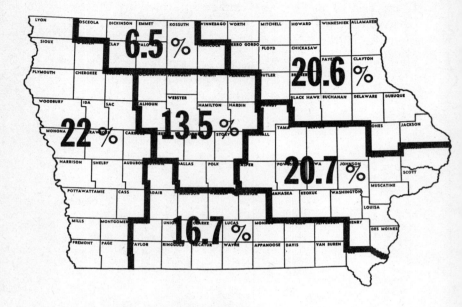

FARM ECONOMIC REGIONS (Iowa)

Heavy black lines outline farm economic regions of
Iowa as defined by the U.S. Department of Agriculture.
Example: The northeast dairy region has 20.6 per cent
of the farms and farm operators in the state. The *Wallaces Farmer* Poll therefore makes 20.6 per cent of its
interviews in this region.

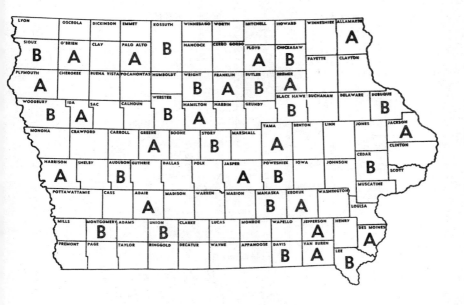

WHERE INTERVIEWS WERE MADE

Interviews were made in counties getting A and B copies as indicated above (for the issue of November 19, 1960). Assignments of A and B interviews are made with relation to the map showing economic regions. For example, interviews in the four A counties in the northeast section make up 20.6 per cent of the inter views in all the A counties. Likewise, interviews in the four B counties in the northeast also make up 20.6 per cent of the interviews in all the B counties.

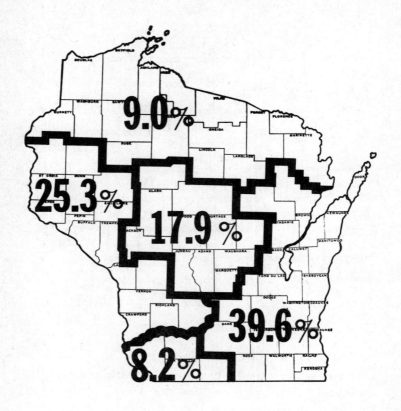

FARM ECONOMIC REGIONS (WISCONSIN)

Heavy black lines outline farm economic regions of Wisconsin as defined by the U.S. Department of Agriculture. *Example*: The southwest region has 8.2 per cent of the farms and farm operators in the state. Therefore the *Wisconsin Agriculturist* Poll interviews in this region were 8.2 per cent of the whole sample.

WHERE INTERVIEWS WERE MADE

Interviews were made in A and B counties (for the issue of October 7, 1961) as indicated above. Note that the southwest region has two A counties and two B counties. Interviews in the two A counties make up 8.2 per cent of the whole A sample. Interviews in the two B counties make up 8.2 per cent of the whole B sample.

16.

Reports on Split Runs and Market Analysis

EXPERIMENTS LIKE THOSE DISCUSSED in this book are eventually summarized in the form of reports. Examples of two classes of the reports follow.

The first is the exact text of a report on a Bovitrin (Merck) advertisement which appeared in the October 3, 1959, issue of *Wisconsin Agriculturist* (See Figures 4.4, 4.5). The second is the exact text of a report analyzing editorial research scores by reader characteristics in the February 4, 1961, issue of *Wallaces Farmer*.

Both reports were prepared by Richard J. Pommrehn, Director of Research for *Wallaces Farmer, Wisconsin Agriculturist* and *Prairie Farmer*.

Bovitrin (Merck) Advertisement
Page 26, October 3, 1959 issue
Wisconsin Agriculturist

PURPOSE OF SURVEY

1. To measure readership of Ad A (test tube illustration) and Ad B (cow illustration).
2. To put questions to readers of the ad to determine sales appeals of different claims for the product.

RESULTS

A detailed report on the survey appears on the following pages. Below is a summary of the high points.

1. The B ad (cow picture) outscored the A ad (test tube picture). Bigger dairymen gave B a marked advantage.
2. Strongest sales appeals were in "hits even remote and hidden pockets of infection," and "returns infected quarter to full production fast."

SAMPLE

The sample was made up of 200 men and 200 women interviewed on their Wisconsin farms. In distribution of interviews by economic sections of the state, the sample compares with census data as follows:

Section	Survey Sample	Census
North	10.7%	11.1%
Central	15.0	17.7
East	40.5	39.5
Southwest	7.8	7.4
West	26.0	24.3
	100.0	100.0

Interviews were made in the following 29 counties:

Barron, Bayfield, Brown, Buffalo, Crawford, Dodge, Dunn, Fond du Lac, Grant, Jackson, Jefferson, Juneau, Kewaunee, La Crosse, Langlade, Manitowoc, Marinette, Polk, Portage, Price, Sauk, Sawyer, St. Croix, Shawano, Taylor, Walworth, Waukesha, Winnebago, Wood.

In distribution of owners and renters, the sample compares with the census as follows:

Tenure	Survey Sample	Census
Owners	86.7%	85.5%
Renters	13.3	14.5
	100.0	100.0

Comparison of data on acreage of crops harvested follows:

	Survey Sample	Census
1–29 acres	6.7%	5.1%
30–99 acres	29.0	28.3
100 acres and up	64.3	66.6
	100.0	100.0

METHOD

Interviewers were sent to designated areas and called on farms where they conducted the usual reader-interest survey of the entire issue. The question asked was: "Did you HAPPEN to see or read anything on this page?" Information obtained by the interviewers was transferred to punch cards by IBM.

1. SPLIT RUN RESULTS

Two ads were exposed to audiences of the same size and character. Ad A showed a picture of test tubes with this head, "New mastitis ointment employs remarkable drug to boost antibiotic efficiency." Ad B showed a picture of a man milking a cow with the head, "To reduce inflammation and let 3 antibiotics attack mastitis." Sales copy also differed.

A and B ads scored as follows:

	Men		Women	
	A	B	A	B
Any This Ad	20%	32%	7%	7%
Head	15	28	3	2
Picture	17	33	6	7
Sales Copy:				
Read Some	11	26	3	2
Read Most	7	18	1	1
Signature	11	20	1	2

(Base is 100 interviews in each group — total of 400).

HOW TO READ: 17 per cent of all men readers of the A issue looked at the picture in the A ad. 33 per cent looked at the picture in the B ad.

This looks as if the B ad were making the best record. But further checks must be made. In the first place, do unchanged ads and copy in this issue in the dairy field score equally in A and B? If unchanged copy scored higher in the B version, then some doubt would be cast on the results above. Three dairy articles preceding the ad averaged scores of 51 Read Some for A and 51 Read Some for B. A nearby dairy ad gave a slight advantage to B. The split, therefore, has passed this test on unchanged copy.

The next step is to see what readers were attracted by the ads. A man with no dairy cows may look at the ad, but this kind of readership will not increase sales.

Let's look first at how many farmers (men) had no cows, how many had from one to nine cows, etc.:

No cows		1–9 cows		10–19 cows		20–29 cows		30 cows and up	
No.	%	No.	%	No.	%	No.	%	No.	%
37	18.8	20	10.1	52	26.4	55	27.9	33	16.8

We will now see how the A and B ads appeal to farmers with different sizes of herds:

	No cows		1–9 cows		10–19 cows		20–29 cows		30 and up	
	A	B	A	B	A	B	A	B	A	B
Any This Ad	%	%	%	%	%	%	%	%	%	%
	23.5	15.0	50.0	50.0	11.5	38.5	19.2	37.9	10.5	28.6
Read Some	11.8	10.0	25.0	37.5	3.8	30.8	15.4	34.5	5.3	21.4

HOW TO READ: Of farmers with 20–29 cows, 34.5 per cent Read Some of the B ad.

The B ad has a commanding lead in the sectors that count.

*   *   *

Another check sorts out farmers who have had mastitis in their herds from those who have had no trouble. The folks who had trouble are more likely to buy treatment for mastitis. This is the way the sample breaks down:

Trouble with mastitis		No trouble	
No.	Per cent	No.	Per cent
87	55.4	70	44.6

Over half of the farmers with dairy cows answered "Yes" to the question: "Have you had any trouble with mastitis in your dairy cattle in 1959?"

The farmers who answered "No trouble in 1959" may have had trouble before or may anticipate trouble in 1960. But the "Yes" group is, at the moment, more important to the advertiser. How did the two groups score?

	Had trouble		No trouble	
	A	B	A	B
Any This Ad	16.7%	47.0%	20.0%	20.0%
Read Some	11.1	41.2	8.9	12.0

HOW TO READ: Of farmers who had trouble with mastitis in 1959, 41.2 per cent Read Some of the B copy.

Again the B ad comes out ahead.

Another check is on farmers who sell Grade A milk and those who do not. Here is the way farmers of each kind responded to the A and B ads.

	Grade A sales		Other	
	A	B	A	B
Any This Ad	4.2%	42.4%	25.0%	30.6%
Read Some	4.2	39.4	13.2	24.2

This again puts B in the lead. Incidentally, 30.5 per cent of the whole sample sell Grade A milk.

What we don't know is which elements in the B ad made the difference. Since picture, head and copy were all changed, we can say no more than that the B layout as a whole is superior to the A layout as a whole. We can guess, on the basis of past experience, that a test tube will attract fewer readers than a cow, but the experiment does not permit us to say how much weight should be given to this.

2. TESTING SALES APPEAL OF DIFFERENT CLAIMS

To each farmer who said he had looked at the ad, a question card was presented. This card said:

Since you looked at or read the Bovitrin ad on mastitis, we'd like to know which items (one or more) of the list below would be most likely to influence you to buy Bovitrin:

1.	It contains a drug which boosts antibiotic action..............	9.6%
2.	It hits even the remote or hidden pockets of infection.........	34.6
3.	It returns infected quarter to full production fast.............	36.5
4.	It reduces udder inflammation and scar tissue...............	5.8
5.	It contains 3 antibiotics....................................	3.8
6.	No opinion any of these...................................	13.5

A and B readers voted alike. The items that got the biggest vote were 2 and 3 above. Since a few voted for more than one item, the total is over 100 per cent.

Editorial Research Report, May 9, 1961
R. J. Pommrehn
Subject: February 4, 1961 issue, *Wallaces Farmer*

EDITORIAL READERSHIP SCORES BY READER CHARACTERISTICS

SCORES OF EDITORIAL ITEMS in the above issue have been broken down by reader characteristics in the usual attempt to determine the types of readers to whom we are appealing.

Both "Read Some" and "Read Most" scores have been used as the basis for cross-tabulations, but only one of these scores was used on any one article. The "Read Most" score was used on articles that seemed likely to receive high readership. "Read Some" scores were used on lower scoring articles. "Read Most" would certainly be the most important measurement, and it may be desirable to use "Read Most" scores as the basis for cross-tabulations on all future articles. However, this report seems to point up a slightly different pattern of readership between "Read Some" and "Read Most," and it indicates that "Read Some" scores cannot be completely overlooked.

Further analysis on this study and future studies might consider the reading habits of so-called "superior" farmers on the theory that we will be writing primarily for these people in the future.

		READ MOST Scores				
		Age Groups			Education Level	
Men Only				50 &	8 yrs.	9 yrs.
Page	Article	21–34	35–49	over	or less	or more
4	Inside Stuff	51.2%	69.3%	61.7%	54.8%	68.0%
6	Washington Report .	23.3	34.7	37.0	27.4	37.6
8–9	Hog Cholera . . .	41.9	40.0	23.5	23.3	40.8
12	Two Price System . .	27.9	33.3	43.2	28.8	41.6
13	Odds 'n Ends . . .	46.5	52.0	50.6	32.9	61.6
16–17	What's Going On in Legislature	11.6	29.3	18.5	16.4	24.8
18	How To Sell Grain Overseas	27.9	34.7	33.3	26.0	36.8
26	Baby Pig Care . . .	60.5	58.7	42.0	45.2	56.0
34–35	Social Security . . .	32.6	26.7	37.0	28.8	34.4
48	Good Records . . .	32.6	34.7	40.7	38.4	35.2
51	Confined Hogs . . .	37.2	41.3	32.1	28.8	40.8
52	Workday Pointers . .	53.5	68.0	46.9	41.1	65.6
62	Poultry Profits . . .	30.2	16.0	18.5	19.2	20.8
64	What Limits Corn Yields?	46.5	53.3	44.4	39.7	52.8
67	Outside Stuff . . .	30.2	48.0	43.2	30.1	50.4
68–69	How Feeds Supply Hog Needs	27.9	22.7	27.2	24.7	25.6
71	Iowa M. D.'s Say . .	16.3	10.7	13.6	13.7	12.8
76	Clean Hog Housing .	37.2	38.7	30.9	27.4	40.0
77	Farm News Briefs . .	20.9	21.3	32.1	21.9	28.8
87	What's Ahead? . . .	46.5	49.3	50.6	42.5	54.4
	Average . . .	35.1	39.1	36.4	30.6	41.4

Average scores by age groups show little or no difference. Farmers with 9 or more years of education were better readers than those with less education. Another report being prepared on this study indicates that younger and middle-aged farmers are those who have been expanding their livestock and poultry operations and plan to continue. Articles on pages 26, 51, 62, and 76, which deal with hog and poultry operations, had their strongest appeal to younger and middle-aged farmers. More general articles appealed to older readers.

| Men Only | | READ SOME Scores | | | | |
| | | Age Groups | | | Education Level | |
Page	Article	21–34	35–49	50 & over	8 yrs. or less	9 yrs. or more
28	Voice of the Farm . .	39.5%	69.3%	60.5%	54.8%	62.4%
30	Passing of Passenger .	11.6	18.7	25.9	. . . . .	. . . . .
36	Safe Driving . . .	32.6	38.7	48.1	. . . . .	. . . . .
37	Heat Lamps . . .	39.5	46.7	48.1	. . . . .	. . . . .
38	Voice of the Farm . .	51.2	69.3	55.6	52.1	64.0
40	Research Points . .	51.2	60.0	58.0	52.1	61.6
42	Water Storage . . .	30.2	36.0	46.9	37.0	40.0
47	Good Credit Risk . .	48.8	45.3	46.9	43.8	48.0
50	Your Family's Good Health	23.3	28.0	21.0	21.9	26.4
53	Visits With Your Vet .	51.2	54.7	54.3	. . . . .	. . . . .
58	Should School Size Be Limited? . . .	39.5	52.0	54.3	42.5	55.0
66	If Your Tax Gets Checked	37.2	53.3	56.8	54.8	48.8
72	Insurance for Hospital Bills . .	25.6	33.3	49.4	39.7	36.8
74	Farm Business Report .	48.8	57.3	48.1	45.2	56.0
86	What's New? . . .	79.1	74.7	61.7	61.6	76.0
	Average . . .	40.6	49.2	49.0	46.0	52.3

The articles, which may be somewhat marginal in reader interest, show on an average a higher appeal to middle-aged and older farmers than to younger farmers. Only "What's New?" showed a much stronger appeal to younger than to older farmers. This may be another indication of the importance of articles that will provide information on how to farm better and more efficiently to the younger group. In contrast with "Read Most" scores by education level which show higher reader interest by those with more education, "Read Some" scores on these articles show that education level made no difference in reader interest. To get a fair test, "Read Some" and "Read Most" scores should be analyzed on the same articles. This may be an indication that readers with less education "sample" an article, while those with more education are more likely to be thorough readers.

		READ MOST Scores		
			Income Level	
Men Only		Under	$5,000	$10,000
Page	Article	$5,000	to $9,999	or more
12	Two Price System	36.4%	32.3%	38.6%
13	Odds 'n Ends	52.3	40.3	59.1
16–17	What's Going On in Legislature . .	15.9	19.4	25.0
34–35	Social Security	40.9	25.8	31.8
48	Good Records	38.6	38.7	31.8
87	What's Ahead?	45.5	48.4	53.4
	Average	38.3	34.2	34.7

		READ SOME Scores		
47	Credit Risk	34.1%	53.2%	46.6%
66	If Your Tax Gets Checked . .	54.5	51.6	47.7
72	Insurance for Hospital Bills . . .	50.0	37.1	31.8
74	Farm Business Report	34.1	56.5	55.7
86	What's New?	59.1	72.6	76.1
	Average	46.4	54.2	51.5

Neither "Read Most" nor "Read Some" scores show any striking differences by income level.

		READ MOST Scores				
			Hogs Marketed in 1960			
Men Only		Less			150 or	
Page	Article	than 50	50–99	100–149	more	None
8–9	Hog Cholera . . .	10.7%	41.7%	30.6%	48.1%	21.9%
26	Baby Pig Care . .	32.1	41.7	52.8	75.3	25.0
51	Confined Hogs . .	14.3	37.5	30.6	53.2	25.0
68–69	How Feeds Supply Hog Needs	17.9	16.7	25.0	36.4	15.6
76	Clean Hog Housing .	14.3	37.5	36.1	51.9	12.5
	Average . .	17.9	35.0	35.0	53.0	20.0

		READ SOME Scores				
37	Heat Lamps . . .	35.7%	41.7%	50.0%	49.4%	40.6%

		READ MOST Scores Laying Flock Size				
Men Only		Less			400 or	
Page	Article	than 100	100–199	200–399	more	None
62	Poultry Profits . .	9.4%	20.0%	30.3%	55.6%	12.3%

		READ MOST Scores Corn Acres Harvested in 1960			
Men Only		1–49	50–74	75 or	
Page	Article	Acres	Acres	more	None
64	What Limits Corn Yields .	46.5%	53.2%	49.0%	16.7%

		READ MOST Scores Crop Acres Harvested in 1960		
Men Only		1–29	30–99	100 Acres
Page	Article	Acres	Acres	or more
18	How To Sell More Grain Overseas	18.2%	19.4%	40.8%

These scores indicate that the larger operators were the best readers.

		READ MOST Scores Source of Income					
Men Only			Beef	Dairy			
Page	Article	Hogs	Cattle	Cattle	Poultry	Crops	Other
53	Visits With Your Vet . . .	57.8%	52.3%	53.7%	35.7%	48.9%	54.5%

		READ SOME Scores Plans To Plant Alfalfa		
Men Only		Do	Don't	
Page	Article	plan to	plan to	Undecided
74	Farm Business Report (Wafered hay)	57.4%	39.2%	50.0%

		READ MOST Scores				
		Age Groups			Education Level	
Women Only				50 &	8 yrs.	9 yrs.
Page	Article	21–34	35–49	over	or less	or more
4	Inside Stuff	55.8%	56.8%	51.4%	43.9%	58.0%
6	Washington Report .	5.8	12.2	13.9	2.4	13.4
34–35	Social Security . . .	11.5	29.7	33.3	17.1	29.3
48	Good Records . . .	34.6	25.7	30.6	22.0	31.8
52	Workday Pointers . .	23.1	37.8	34.7	29.3	34.4
54	Light Up the Living Room . . .	50.0	48.6	52.8	51.2	50.3
56	Cookery Corner . .	75.0	85.1	75.0	70.7	81.5
57	Country Air . . .	51.9	59.5	59.7	. . . .	. . . .
61	Personal Notes . . .	44.2	58.1	55.6	. . . .	. . . .
62	Poultry Profits . . .	11.5	13.5	20.8	22.0	14.0
67	Outside Stuff . . .	30.8	39.2	40.3	41.5	36.9
70	Start Garden Plans Early	44.2	41.9	37.5	. . . .	. . . .
71	Iowa M. D.'s Say . .	32.7	29.7	29.2	19.5	33.8
	Average . . .	36.2	41.4	41.1	32.0	38.3

| Women Only | | READ SOME Scores | | | | |
| | | Age Groups | | | Education Level | |
Page	Article	21–34	35–49	50 & over	8 yrs. or less	9 yrs. or more
28	Voice of the Farm . .	32.7%	50.0%	45.8%	29.3%	48.4%
30	Passing of Passenger .	21.2	23.0	26.6	....	....
36	Safe Driving . . .	48.1	36.5	44.4	....	....
38	Voice of the Farm . .	42.3	56.8	45.8	43.9	50.3
40	Research Points . .	23.1	28.4	36.1	31.7	29.9
42	Water Storage . . .	17.3	20.3	15.3	7.3	21.0
47	Credit Risk	32.7	32.4	27.8	14.6	35.7
50	Your Family's Good Health	42.3	47.3	45.8	26.8	50.3
58	Should School Size Be Limited?	53.8	66.2	65.3	56.1	64.3
66	If Your Tax Gets Checked	32.7	44.6	50.0	31.7	47.1
72	Insurance for Hospital Bills	51.9	52.7	63.9	46.3	59.2
86	What's New? . . .	32.7	27.0	29.2	29.3	29.9
	Average . . .	35.9	40.4	41.3	31.7	43.6

Average "Read Some" and "Read Most" scores by age groups for women on selected items throughout the magazine show the same pattern — a fairly even level of interest with a possible slight advantage for middle-aged and older women. Women with the most education were the best readers.

| Women Only | | READ MOST Scores | | | | |
| | | Laying Flock Size | | | | |
Page	Article	Less than 100	100–199	200–399	400 or more	None
62	Poultry Profits . .	18.0%	9.7%	27.8%	31.8%	3.6%

Women Only		READ MOST Scores Income Level		
Page	Article	Under $5,000	$5,000 to $9,999	$10,000 or more
13	Odds 'n Ends	17.1%	22.2%	25.3%
34–35	Social Security	29.3	27.8	21.3
48	Good Records	29.3	31.9	28.0
54	Light Up the Living Room . . .	48.8	48.6	54.7
	Average	31.1	32.6	32.3

		READ SOME Scores		
47	Credit Risk	24.4%	38.9%	26.7%
66	If Your Tax Gets Checked . . .	48.8	43.1	41.3
72	Insurance for Hospital Bills . . .	48.8	55.6	60.0
86	What's New?	34.1	27.8	33.3
	Average	39.0	41.3	40.3

Average scores by income levels were the same on these articles, but individual articles did not all follow the pattern.

Women Only		READ MOST Scores Family Size		
Page	Article	1 or 2 in family	3 in family	4 or more
54	Light Up the Living Room . . .	47.3%	60.6%	50.0%
56	Cookery Corner	78.2	72.7	81.3
70	Start Garden Plans Early . . .	38.2	33.3	45.5
71	Iowa M. D.'s Say	29.1	27.3	33.0
	Average	48.2	48.5	52.5

On an average, family size had little, if any, effect on reader interest in these articles.

Notes to Citations

CHAPTER 1

(1) Advertising Research Foundation: Study No. 4, *Wallaces Farmer and Iowa Homestead (Continuing Study of Farm Publications).* September 20, 1947.

(2) Statistical Laboratory, Iowa State University: "InFARMation Please," No. 1, 1947; No. 2, 1951; No. 3, 1955. *Wallaces Farmer,* Des Moines, Iowa.

(3) Kearl, Bryant, "The Non-Reader in a Magazine Readership Survey." *Journalism Quarterly,* Fall, 1957.

(4) Lyman, Howard B., "Flesch Count and Readership of Articles." *Journal of Applied Psychology,* February, 1949.

(5) Ludwig, Merrit C., "Hard Words and Human Interest; Their Effects on Readership." *Journalism Quarterly,* June, 1949.

(6) Flesch, Rudolph, The Art of Readable Writing. *Harpers,* 1949.

CHAPTER 2

(1) Savage, Job K., Jr.: *Effectiveness of the Midland Cooperator.* Farmers Cooperative Service, U.S. Department of Agriculture; October 1, 1956.

(2) Advertising Research Foundation, *loc. cit.*

CHAPTER 3

(1) Pommrehn, Richard J., "Black and White Versus Color." Research Department Report, *Wallaces Farmer,* 1956.

(2) Freeman, Chester H.: *Attention and Retention Value of Color.* Communication Bulletin No. 1, Cornell University, October, 1960.

CHAPTER 4

(1) For a helpful discussion of these and many other points in photography, *see* Fox and Kerns: *Creative News Photography*.

(2) Pommrehn, Richard J.: *Split-run Readership Test as a Means of Increasing Ad Readership*. MSS. M.A. thesis, Drake University, 1953.

(3) Research Department, Curtis Publishing Company: Magazine Editorial Research, Curtis Publishing Company, 1956.

(4) These and other statements at the end of chapters have too dogmatic and self-assured an air. Yet it is boring to say every time, "This conclusion is based on several experiments which seem to me to indicate a tendency in the direction of the statement here presented. I recognize that further experiments may change the picture. I also admit that subjective bias (often unrecognized as such) has probably played a part in the framing of this recommendation. In short, this is as much as I think I know today. It is not the last word on the subject, but it is probably a better word than I could produce if I hadn't run these tests."

CHAPTER 5

(1) Murphy, Donald R., "Page Position and Readership on a Farm Magazine." *Journalism Quarterly*, Fall, 1957.

CHAPTER 6

(1) Felstenhausen, Herman: MSS. Department of Agricultural Journalism, University of Wisconsin, 1961.

CHAPTER 7

(1) Discussion of the relationship of editorial copy to advertisements is particularly sharp in the field of television. While most publications reserve for themselves the right to select all editorial copy, many television advertisers insist on controlling the programs in which their advertisements appear. Associated Press (September 27, 1961) reported a hearing before the Federal Communications Commission and noted that one director of advertising said his company "reviewed scripts for TV to make sure what we were doing and what we were saying were in the best interests of our corporation." Another advertiser took a different view and said that his company "had no voice in the subject matter, production techniques and casting of plays, but left those matters to the producers." This latter position is, of course, the point of view of most publishers and editors of magazines.

(2) Murphy, Donald R., "Position Next to Dull or Dandy Matter," *Printers' Ink*, August 24, 1951.

CHAPTER 8

(1) For more discussion on this point, *see* Murphy, Donald R., "Farm Paper Study Goes Beyond Readership, Checks Ability To Reach Buyers." *Advertising Age,* May 29, 1961.

CHAPTER 10

(1) The need of measuring "areas of national ignorance" was pointed out by Elmo Roper, in *Fortune,* February, 1942. He said, "During my eight years of asking the common man questions about what he thinks and what he wants I have often been surprised and disappointed to discover that he has less information than we think he should have about some question we consider important. . . I believe the first duty (of public opinion research) is to explore the areas of public ignorance somewhat as we have tried to do in the survey on labor. . . . By experimenting further now in finding out what things people misunderstand or don't know, we shall be able to discount 'public opinion' that stands on a base of ignorance. And we shall be able to define in most specific terms the work to be done by our educators and thought leaders, now and in the future."

CHAPTER 11

(1) Statistical Laboratory, Iowa State University, *loc. cit.*

CHAPTER 12

(1) Murphy, Donald R., "Do Farmers Believe What They Read?" *Journalism Quarterly,* Winter, 1960.

CHAPTER 13

(1) Johnson, Glenn, "New Knowledge of Decision Making Process." *Journal of Farm Economics,* December, 1958.

(2) On this point, Charles K. Ramond, Technical Director, Advertising Research Foundation, commented in an address (January 26, 1960) before the Toronto chapter of the American Marketing Association. Raymond said that "fear of experimentation is a natural distaste for any approach which appears to reduce experienced executive judgment to mathematical formulae. This is mainly due to a failure to understand the true function of the experimental method. It can never replace judgement; it can only narrow the range of uncertainty within which such judgment must always act. The question is not whether decisions can be better made by computers or by human beings. The question is whether human beings can make decisions better with or without the help of computers and experimentation."

CHAPTER 14

(1) Hinkle, Lawrence E., Jr., "Communist Manipulation of Behavior." *Science*, June 16, 1961.
(2) Boulding, Kenneth E., "Reflections on Poverty." Address before National Conference on Social Welfare, Minneapolis, Minnesota, May 15, 1961.

SURVEY METHODS

(1) Light on the makeup of the subscription list of *Wallaces Farmer* came from three name-matching studies conducted by the U.S. Bureau of the Census. In the 1954 study, for instance, 1937 names of subscribers were matched with census data secured for these same names. The census study indicated that subscribers to *Wallaces Farmer* had slightly larger farms (190.0 acres to 176.5 acres) than the average Iowa farmer. The Iowa farm subscriber also had somewhat more valuable land and buildings ($39,738 to $36,090).
(2) Jones, Robert L., "Methodological Improvements in Readership Data Gathering." *Journalism Quarterly*, Summer, 1953.

Books To Read

BOOKS LISTED BELOW have been useful in our editorial research. Also useful have been articles in *Advertising Age, American Journal of Sociology, Journal of Applied Psychology, Journal of Farm Economics, Journalism Quarterly, Public Opinion Quarterly* and *Printers' Ink*.

Adorno, T. W.: *Authoritarian Personality*. Harpers, N. Y., 1950.

Allport, Gordon W.: *Nature of Prejudice*. Doubleday, N.Y., 1954.

Allport, Gordon W., and Postman, Leo: *The Psychology of Rumor*. Henry Holt, N. Y., 1947.

Anderson, Harold H., and Anderson, Gladys L.: *An Introduction to Projective Techniques*. Prentice-Hall, N. Y., 1951.

Berelson, Bernard R., Lazarsfeld, Paul F., and McPhee, William N.: *Voting: A Study of Opinion Formation in a Presidential Campaign*. University of Chicago Press, Chicago, 1954.

Blankenship, Albert B.: *How To Conduct Consumer and Opinion Research*. Harper & Brothers, N. Y., 1946.

Campbell, Angus, Gurin, Gerald, and Miller, Warren E.: *The Voter Decides*. Row, Peterson, White Plains, N. Y., 1954.

Cantril, Hadley: *Gauging Public Opinion*. Princeton University Press, Princeton, 1944.

Charnley, Mitchell V., and Converse, Blair: *Magazine Writing and Editing*. Gordon, N. Y., 1938.

Fox, Rodney, and Kerns, Robert: *Creative News Photography*. Iowa State University Press, Ames, 1961.

Hovland, Carl I., Janis, Irving L., and Kelley, Harold H.: *Communication and Persuasion*. Yale University Press, New Haven, 1953.

Hovland, Carl I., Mandell, Wallace, Campbell, Enid H., Brock, Timothy, Luchins, Abraham S., Cohen, Arthur R., McGuire, William J., Janis, Irving L., Feierabend, Rosalind L., and Anderson, Norman H.: *The Order of Presentation in Persuasion*. Yale University Press, New Haven, 1957.

Hyman, Herbert H.: *Interviewing in Social Research*. University of Chicago Press, Chicago, 1954.

Katz, Elihu, and Lazarsfeld, Paul F.: *Personal Influence*. Free Press, Glencoe, Ill., 1955.

Klapper, Joseph T.: *The Effects of Mass Communication.* Free Press, Glencoe, Ill., 1960.

Klare, George R., and Buck, Byron: *Know Your Reader.* Hermitage House, N. Y., 1954.

Lasswell, Harold D., and Leites, Nathan: *The Language of Politics.* Stewart, N. Y., 1949.

Lazarsfeld, Paul F., Berelson, Bernard, and Gaudet, Hazel: *The People's Choice.* Duell, Sloan and Pearce, N. Y., 1944.

Lazarsfeld, Paul F., and Rosenberg, Morris: *The Language of Social Research.* Free Press, Glencoe, Ill., 1955.

Lazarsfeld, Paul F., and Stanton, Frank: *Communications Research,* 1948–1949. Harper & Brothers, N. Y., 1949.

Lerner, Daniel, and Lasswell, Harold D.: *Policy Sciences: Recent Development in Scope and Method.* Stanford University Press, Stanford, Calif., 1951.

Lionberger, Herbert F.: *Adoption of New Ideas and Practices.* Iowa State University Press, Ames, 1962.

Mainland, Donald: *Tables for Use With Binomial Samples.* New York University, New York, 1956.

Mencken, H. L.: *The American Language.* Supplement One; Supplement Two. A. Knopf, N. Y., 1936, 1945, 1948.

Osgood, Charles E., Suci, George J., and Tannenbaum, Percy H.: *The Measurement of Meaning.* University of Illinois Press, Urbana, 1957.

Schramm, Wilbur: *Communications in Modern Society.* University of Illinois Press, Urbana, 1948.

Schramm, Wilbur: *Mass Communications.* University of Illinois Press, Urbana, 1949.

Schramm, Wilbur: *The Process and Effects of Mass Communication.* University of Illinois Press, Urbana, 1955.

Smith, M. Brewster, Bruner, Jerome S., and White, Robert W.: *Opinions and Personality.* John Wiley & Sons, Inc., N. Y., 1956.

Smith, George Horsley: *Motivation Research in Advertising and Marketing.* McGraw-Hill Book Co., Inc., N. Y., 1954.

Stouffer, Samuel A.: *The American Soldier,* Vols. 1–4. Princeton University Press, Princeton, 1949.

Stouffer, Samuel A.: *Communism, Conformity, and Civil Liberties.* Doubleday & Company, Inc., N. Y., 1955.

Waples, Douglas, Berelson, Bernard, and Bradshaw, Franklyn R.: *What Reading Does to People.* University of Chicago Press, Chicago, 1940.

Index